TO LARRY — THE
GREATEST CAT OF
THEM ALL *

ABOVE THE FRAY
Customer Service

BY PAUL KAREM

Some answers to
America's
customer service disaster.

Presenting
three steps
for developing great
customer service in
your organization.

* BESIDES DICKY LYONS

To Sandra –
My love, my friend, my advisor, my mentor,
my inspiration, my coach, my buddy.

"Run with it!"

ABOVE THE FRAY

PART ONE:
AMERICA'S CUSTOMER SERVICE DISASTER

PART TWO:
MANAGING YOURSELF

PART THREE:
BUILDING A TEAM

ABOVE THE FRAY

PART FOUR:
WINNING THE EXTERNAL CUSTOMER

APPENDIX:
EMPLOYEE CONTRACTS &
CUSTOMER SERVICE REVIEW

PART ONE: AMERICA'S CUSTOMER SERVICE DISASTER

Some examples of bad self-management and bad team-management that have led to loss of respect for the customer.

As a customer YOU have experienced some or all of what follows.

AMERICA'S CUSTOMER SERVICE DISASTER

We have lost respect for the customer in America. It has become the norm for service providers to be inconsiderate and unhelpful. The customer, internal and external, has fallen to the wayside of the phone tree, voice mail, the presumed pursuit of profit, and the attitude of those who are hired to provide the customer service.

Being respectful, courteous and sensitive to the customer has somehow become confused with being submissive and subservient. It is no longer considered dignified to assist and help the customer – it is now considered groveling or humiliating. At some point, "I am not a waiter" and "I am not your slave" and "I don't have to do that for you" have taken the place of "how can I please you?" A basic, human desire to please has been replaced with an unattractive, thin-skinned, self-righteousness.

We give nicknames to certain periods of our history. Some of these include the "Roaring Twenties", the "Gilded Age", the "Victorian Age". One day the nickname given to our particular era may be "the Selfish Age" or the "Unhelpful Age." Whatever our era is called, it sure will be great when it has finally run its course.

Here are just a few examples from our "Unhelpful Age" in American customer service:

• **"This is not my table."** Truly the most unhelpful phrase heard in the food service industry. We have all experienced such rudeness – numerous times. We cringe as we receive this brush-off after we have made a reasonable request to a member of the restaurant's wait staff.

How did we ever get to the point where we customers tolerate this rudeness? More importantly, why does the owner of a restaurant allow members of the wait staff to speak to customers like this?

• **"Open the door!"** Have you ever been to a retail store 5-10 minutes or so before their "official" opening time? If you have, did you notice people walking around in the store acting like they don't see you? Why won't they acknowledge your presence? Aren't they happy to see that they have customers? They are in there to sell you something and you have just arrived to buy it. Therefore...why won't they open the door?

If there's a good reason, then someone could at least approach the door and say something like, "We'll be with you in a minute."

• **"Please hold, all representatives are busy."** Recently, I called my cellular phone service provider to get some clarification on my bill. Instead of receiving helpful service, I got a recording that said, "Please hold, all representatives are busy."

While waiting on infinite "hold" I pondered the ultimate irony – I called the *phone company* and there was no one to *answer the phone*!

• **"You can close this deal if you cancel another one."** This really happened! I ran a mortgage company. We were closing a mortgage and had pre-sold the loan to another mortgage company. We had already booked the loan to close on a Thursday and it was only Tuesday.

The closer for the company that had bought the loan did not want to prepare another closing package. She told my staff: "I will prepare the closing package (which is a matter of a few finger pushes on a keyboard) if you cancel one of your other loans."

In other words: "I will pick a new barrel of apples for you if you let the other barrel rot." The single dumbest thing I have ever heard in the mortgage business. We never closed another loan with that company – which is no longer in business.

It goes from the top to the bottom. I once worked for a company where the single *least* important call the

CEO could get was from an employee. You knew that because of the unhelpful way the call was received and handled. However, I also once worked for a company where the single **most** important call the CEO could get was from an employee. You knew that because of the way the call was received and handled. The first company does not exist anymore. The second company is flourishing.

We have lost respect for the customer in America.

The customer, internal and external, has fallen to the wayside

BEWARE OF
SMILING FACES

Recently, I went into the offices of my cellular phone service provider to resolve a problem with my cell phone. The voice mail icon on my phone screen would not go away even after I had deleted all of my voice mails. It was annoying me and I decided to get it taken care of.

When I walked into the store I was overcome with comfort and calm, because the posters on the store's walls and hanging from its ceiling, assured me that my every concern would be quickly and deftly handled.

What could be more reassuring than seeing a poster of a young man resting on a picnic blanket and smiling because of the wonderful cell phone in his hand and the proclamation under the poster – "Your satisfaction is our passion"? Or the poster next to it that portrayed a woman laughing gleefully with her young child in a total cell-phone induced state of phone rapture?

Everyone portrayed in the posters is totally overcome with pleasure using their cell phones! Not only are these posters reassuring and comforting, but the store is also adorned with guarantees and bonus contracts – sales promises and pledges – testimonials and displays of customer service awards! How can anything go wrong?

But something can go wrong. It went wrong when I walked over to the customer service window and talked to the customer service representative. Apparently, the customer service representative had not had a chance to review the posters. She wasn't in tune with the phone-induced happiness pictured throughout the store. More than that, I think I can say with confidence that *"my satisfaction was **not** her passion."* I experienced an obvious **disconnect** between the helpful, encouraging message in the posters and her attitude.

When I explained my problem with the voice mail icon, she began to take me through the basics of erasing voice mails, which I told her repeatedly, I had already done! This **customer hatred representative** (CHR) was in an "ignore the customer" daze and did not even hear what I was saying. When it was clear that "I wasn't getting it," she disgustedly turned to her co-hort, the technical representative and blurted out, "Can you get this guy straightened out?"

In a matter of minutes I had gone from being a happy man at a picnic – to a *guy who needed straightening out.* The claims on the posters and the company's supposed dedication to the customer had been completely negated by a customer service rep who behaved as if her title should more accurately be *gatekeeper.* She believed she was there to protect the company, *not to satisfy* customers.

You have to wonder how the posters got there in the first place. Does an established company just go to an advertising agency and say to them "Make up some posters of happy people so we can trick everybody"?

I am not telling you this to pick on the cell phone provider. I am telling you this because these CHRs, **Customer Hatred Representatives,** are being mass-produced in businesses across America! There is a serious disconnect between the satisfying level of service the companies advertise and the level of service that their employees provide.

Companies now make **claims that they and their employees are simply not in sync with.** Like the maddening recording you get when you call the cable TV company to lodge a complaint. You are on hold for 45 minutes while you listen to a recording that tells you how important you are as a customer!

What is going on? If you are so important to them why can't they answer the phone? You are put on marathon hold, and you get the recording that says, "this call may be recorded for quality-control purposes."

The **DISCONNECT** in full force.
The posters say one thing, but the
Customer Hatred Rep says another.

Quality control my foot! Who is going to assess the level of quality? **The CHR – the Customer Hatred Representative?**

If you walk into a business that is adorned with posters of smiling customers, get out immediately. Get out now! Somewhere, somehow, **business in America has pulled off a** *disconnect* **between their claims of customer service and their performance.**

> **There is a serious DISCONNECT between the satisfying level of service companies advertise and the level of service that their employees provide.**

PARKING FOR CUSTOMERS ONLY

The lengths that businesses will go to today to insult people and run off customers are truly amazing. They just don't think!

I have a regular stop on the way to work every morning at Starbucks – for a large coffee with a shot of espresso.

Next to the Starbucks is a furniture store parking lot. The coffee customers park there in the morning before the furniture store opens. To make sure nothing terrible happens, the furniture store has adorned its parking lot with serious warning signs that declare: *WARNING— Parking for furniture store customers ONLY.* Not very neighborly, but the story gets worse.

One morning, I arrived at my coffee stop a little later than usual, and the furniture store had opened. I pulled my car into a *furniture store* spot.

As I got out of the car, out came the man from the furniture store. He admonished me for being so careless as to park in a furniture store parking spot. His first comment set the tone for the next five minutes – "Can't you read?" How does one respond to such a question? Then he exhorted, "If you could read, you could see that this parking is for furniture store customers only!"

My response to him should have knocked him completely off this track. "Sir," I said in my most polite tone, "I am a furniture store customer. I have bought many items from your store and have been a long and trusted customer." Still determined to straighten me out, he continued with more ranting dialogue – going on and on about the sanctity of the furniture store's parking spaces!

He just never got what I was trying to tell him. There were maybe 75 open parking spots in the furniture store area, and one thing about all this really struck me. This guy was putting more effort into the management of the parking spaces than into developing a customer. In fact, he was really excited about giving a faithful customer grief! Unfortunately, this backwards behavior seems to be a growing hobby in business today.

Why does the negative approach get the better of the positive? Why is that? Why was that guy so motivated to run out the door and give me hell? Why didn't he realize that I was a valued customer – especially after I told him so – and use his common sense?

How did the furniture guy catch the same customer service disease as the customer hatred representative at the cellular phone service center? Today, there just seems to be something about the chance to be negative that overwhelms the chance to be positive.

Whatever the reason, the negative epidemic is out there and we have to guard against it. This is an infectious disease.

Here are **two thoughts** I had after this experience:

1. The man who expelled me from the furniture store parking lot will never put that much effort into a sale or into taking care of a customer. Bet on it.

2. Even when I told the guy I was a customer, he continued to dwell on the parking issue. All I was doing was giving him the opportunity to be a better business-man – to cater to a customer – to build his business!

> **Why don't American companies today use every opportunity to cater to customers? After all – it's a proven way to build business.**

Discreet
Customer Contempt

Sometimes you get the feeling that service people are not all that interested in being helpful. You know the type.

> It could be the bank teller whose head drops down immediately when you have selected her window instead of one of the other open windows.

> It could be the waiter, who walks up to your table, takes out a pencil and order pad but doesn't bother to greet you.

> It could be the guy with the chip on his shoulder in the auto service department of your car dealership. He has an attitude problem. He seems resentful of the fact that you drive a nice

car! It bores him to have to deal with someone who knows so little about cars when he knows so much.

It could be the inept mortgage guy who forgets to tell you your loan has a prepayment penalty and now he won't return your call.

It could be the customer service rep you are on the phone with at the health insurance company. You can't get your situation settled because she just keeps repeating her script like a robot.

Remember the movie *Meet the Parents*? Do you recall the airline ticket agent who would not let the hapless, main character of the movie board the plane although there were no other people – not one – in the boarding gate? If you don't think that ticket agent is based on real life experience, you must not get out much.

These unhelpful people are upon us in droves in customer service jobs that do not warrant their discouraging behavior. However, their behavior is easily defined. I call it **Discreet Customer Contempt**. They actually have contempt for the customer, and it manifests itself in their behavior. They try to hide their contempt, but they can't. Let me repeat: **They try to hide it but they can't.**

How did we get to the point where **Discreet Customer Contempt** exists in customer service settings? The answer is not clear but I've identified two likely causes:

NUMBER 1

The disconnect – defined as follows – The lack of connection between a company or business that claims to provide service but allows its employees to behave otherwise.

The disconnect has become commonplace in business settings. The disconnect results when a company utilizes advertising that it believes will be effective with customers, but that advertising, and the people who are supposed to embrace and actualize the claims in the advertising, are never exposed to each other. The ad agency does not know the people in the company, and the people in the company don't know anything about the claims in the ads. The result of this is lackluster, unhelpful behavior on the job. So the disconnect happens because it is allowed to happen.

NUMBER 2

Thin-skinned self-righteousness: Somehow today, it has become personally demeaning to extend yourself with a customer. It is seemingly a violation of a service provider's dignity. It is now considered undignified to go out of your way to help people – it is considered too humiliating.

Other cultures do not have this thin-skinned self-righteousness polluting their customer service. In many other cultures, service jobs – such as waiter – are respected, skilled professions. In such cultures, a waiter is professionally pleased to be of service.

**Why, in America today, has it become
undignified to be helpful?**

Why is it that being extremely helpful to customers is experienced as a personal indignity and compromising to the customer service provider? Why can't people be as helpful as the Ruths of the world and feel good about it? (We'll learn more about Ruth later.)

In our culture, a wait-staff job is often a step to another job. Many employees seem to think this means that you don't really have to be as courteous as you might be since "this is not my real job." That is ignorant thinking because that employee is giving up the chance to be great at something, even if he or she later pursues a different vocation.

How many times have you had a waiter roll his or her eyes at you because you changed or corrected an order?

How many times have you felt like you were wasting a customer service representative's precious time with your "ignorant" questions?

The disconnect and thin-skinned self-righteousness are poisoning customer service in America.

Is there a better way? If we all agree that we're living in a toxic stew of negative customer service, what can we do about it? Why might a company today decide to distinguish itself by providing truly great customer service?

In the next section, Part Two,
we'll look at making some steps
toward improvement
by starting with ourselves.

Then we'll see how
we can build a successful team
and motivate others.

PART TWO:

MANAGING
YOURSELF

If you want to make your company
or your business greater –

LOOK INSIDE YOURSELF.

LEVELS OF ATTRACTIVENESS TO CUSTOMERS

We have seen that American business currently wallows in a customer service disaster. But, what does that mean to you? As a customer, you suffer with it as we all do. But, as a sales professional, manager or motivated employee, this situation provides you with an opportunity. **Becoming outstanding in customer service will distinguish you and your company, develop a satisfied customer base, and promote your success.**

In this section, Part Two, we're going to concentrate on you. Your attitude toward your industry and your customer sets the stage for your company's approach to service. If you are a model of good customer service, not only will you gain and keep your own customers, but you will also inspire your co-workers and staff.

There is a progression that can be achieved in terms of how your customers react to you. It is the ultimate in terms of achieving success in your industry. It is the ability to be sought out by the customer. You might not think you can achieve this, but I assure you it can be done. I know what I'm talking about because I did it, and I have watched and observed others do it.

Generally speaking, what one is trying to achieve while building customer service or sales success is simply to be **recognized as a respectable source** for whatever product or service you represent. This is the **first level of achievement** and is a great place to be. It shows you've done your job in an ethical, professional manner and people want to do business with you. You've carried yourself well and people are comfortable associating with you.

The **second level of achievement** occurs when you are **recognized as one of the better sources, or as a leader in your field**. You've had some kind of success that can be documented. Now you have started to separate yourself from your competition. Your market share rank has gone up. Your customer service reviews indicate the customer is happy with your level of service. Business is good and the bank account shows it.

At the **third level**, you are **recognized as the best source in your field**. You've progressed through the first two levels. You cannot progress in the arena of great customer service if you don't do it through the progression of levels. That is the entire basis of this book which embraces three levels of self and team management. But one cannot be achieved without the preceding one being done correctly.

It is much like building a house. What good is a beautiful kitchen if it has been built over a faulty foundation that is about to cave in?

Let's review the first three levels of attractiveness to the customer:
1. You are recognized as a respectable source.
2. You are recognized as one of the best sources.
3. You are successful to the extent that you are recognized as the best.

Believe it or not there is one more level:
You are sought out by the external customer – THEY CALL YOU TO DO BUSINESS!
Again, the way to achieve this is by progression. You have to achieve the first three steps and then the amazing fourth step will develop as a result!

People in the customer service arena are in a highly competitive environment. Actually, all you have to sell is service. No one really has a product or service that is a quantum leap above and beyond the competition.

In residential mortgage lending, a business in which I have extensive experience, every single person or company talks about how great their service is. It is a standard claim – *"We have the best service."* But how can one stand behind that claim? How can you quantify for customers that your service is the best? When you can do that, and tell your story to your customer base, you've struck gold. In my company, we decided to carve out a mission statement – a company slogan – that quantified why our customer service was better. We decided that slogan to be: *"No voice mail during office hours."*

Customers want personal service. Nobody wants to go through the aggravating phone-tree prompts that often result in the chosen option generating yet another maddening recorded message. Our bet was that the other lenders would not be willing to challenge their  systems and personnel to meet the requirements of such an unyielding standard.

Guess what? We were right on both counts. The bottom line is that it worked, and it energized potential customers to seek us out. The external customer came after us because we drew a line in the sand, and put our money where our mouth is in terms of our customer service claim!

But wait a minute! This didn't happen because an ad agency thought of a clever saying for us. We had to progress through the first three levels of attractiveness to customers. We got to the point where we understood our customers' needs well enough that we gained awareness that our new policy was wanted in the marketplace.

GIVE THE CUSTOMER
THE QUALITY
SERVICE THEY WANT,
AND THEY WILL
SEEK YOU OUT.

ABOVE THE FRAY

The biggest compliment I ever received in business was from one of my salespeople who told me I was **above the fray** in comparison to the other people we competed against.

Those words – **above the fray** – resonated in my ears when he said it. I have always tried to carry myself in a manner that exudes confidence. If you have a sense of what the customer wants, you know that the first thing the customer wants to see is someone who is confident in their profession.

When you think of being above the fray, certain athletes come to mind. These athletes seem to be unconcerned about the competition and do not lose their poise under any circumstance. Remember the tennis great, Björn Borg. He was completely impervious to annoyances – like missing an easy shot or getting a lousy call from an umpire. What an impressive way to carry yourself! Think about the messages he was sending out. He showed no emotion or hysterics over a blown call by an official, while at the same time his opponent was going insane over a call that didn't go his way.

What messages are being sent? Could it be that the opponent gets intimidated by the mere cool of someone who carries himself so assuredly? Maybe the message to the opponent is "I'm so certain of my skill and resolve to beat you, that no outside influence can stop that from happening." Wouldn't that be a little unnerving to the foe? Which is more effective? – carrying yourself in Björn's manner or acting like a crybaby over every call and unforced error?

Can you see where this approach has a carryover into the business environment? Do you know people who crybaby over misfortune in the business setting? Do you work with others who carry themselves with cool self-assuredness and a confident business manner? More importantly, which one of these is you? If you were the customer, which one of these types would you rather have handling your account? I don't think that question is too tough to answer.

A bigger question is this: Which one of these types would you rather work with or have as a teammate? The **above the fray performers** carry the highest level of competitiveness, but this drive is indistinguishable to the human eye. They do not enter into today's popular arena of negative discussion, do not descend to the level of their less-honorable foes, do not engage in negative dialogue about their peers, and hold **NO ONE** accountable for their success but themselves.

Trade industry gatherings like the Homebuilders Association, or the Florists Association or the State Bankers Association, or the Automobile Dealers Association are intriguing events. Here you are, up close and personal over a martini or a steak, with the people you compete against day to day.

Here you meet old friends and young bucks who are all fired up about taking away your book of business. I think it is very important to carry yourself in a certain manner at such gatherings, in an **above the fray** manner. Throw your competitors off-balance by addressing them with the same level of warmth that you would a prospective external customer.

The benefits of an **above the fray** attitude are:

> • You are acting and presenting yourself in a high-class and professional manner.

> • You are, in a subtle way, impressing others in your industry who may come to you someday for a position.

> • You are knocking off balance the doomsayers and professional malcontents who are always knocking everyone else and looking for some way to make excuses for their shortcomings.

You can gain an inner strength with an **above the fray** attitude – like Björn did. **I have never worried about the competition, only about my performance.**

> **Develop an Above the Fray attitude.**
>
> **Never worry about the competition, only about your own performance**

THE PROFESSIONAL DOOMSAYER

It takes more time and energy to foster a negative attitude about something than you could ever expend on smart, diligent, goal-oriented activity. I mean you really have to work at being a sourpuss.

The real estate business in general (meaning realtors, mortgage originators, builders, and all the related industries) seems to attract a lot of these doomsayers. Maybe I'm wrong – maybe this industry is not the world capital of negativism, but sometimes it sure seems like it – like everybody is always in a bad mood and talking about how awful everything is!

On the other hand, this kind of behavior is starting to become the American way. It is becoming the fashionable way to act. I have to fight it in my business and my family life everyday! My children come home with doomsayer stories from friends and teachers! All the latest and newest reasons why things are going bad and all the latest reasons why they should fall into the trap and be miserable, too.

Here's some doom-saying I've heard in my career:

• **"Everybody says business is slow**. There is no reason to go out and make sales calls. The cost of energy is killing the economy!"

• **"Rates are going up**, so no wonder we aren't writing any new loans!" (The doomsayers invoke this when rates are one four-millionth higher than they were 60 days prior.)

• **"This city is backward!** Traffic is all messed up. No way we can have a dynamic business in this town!"

• **"Nobody does any business this time of year** anyway. Let's go have a cold beer."

• **"The competition is giving it away and our prices are too high.** Let's go play nine." This is a sampling of the kind of poison you hear in every business. Choose not to buy into or believe any of it – even if it has some validity. Most of this is just a way for some people to manifest their own doubts and reluctance to stretch past a barrier.

This is what this whole book is about: Getting past behavior barriers like doom-saying, and getting yourself and your staff to a different, more productive place. Set yourself apart from these doom-saying characters (there will always be a lot of them to choose from) and their thinking.

Never hold anyone, anything, or any circumstance accountable for your success but YOURSELF. If you make a rule that you and you alone are responsible for your success then you will dismiss from your experience the constant energy drain that comes with finding and locating places and people to blame for your short-falls.

If you stay clear of doom saying, you will be an energy efficient machine and accomplish more in a 40-hour workweek than the doomsayer will in a month of moaning.

Believe it. I know it, because I, like you, find it so easy to fall into the trap of the professional doomsayer. It's addicting and comforting. But in the end it's kind of like arguing with the referee after the call has already been made. It can only hurt if you don't get over it and go forward with the resolve to do something positive.

Even if you can avoid this negative behavior only 75% of the time, your production will soar.

When business is *really bad* for valid reasons – I will concede that there is such a thing as a valid reason for a bad business environment…but rarely – **your market share will increase.**

When business kicks back in, you will get a bonus! **YOU WILL TAKE AN IMMEDIATE STEP TO**

THE NEXT LEVEL OF PRODUCTION. Star sales-people get the majority of the business when the business climate is tough and the customer is asking tough questions.

In golf, a skillful, tough competitor would rather meet a challenger in a championship match on the toughest course. It is similar in the business environment. For example, in the mortgage business in 2003, when rates were at all time lows, everybody and his brother were making a living writing refinance mortgages. Later, rates adjusted and that windfall was gone. Meanwhile, our market share at Paul Karem Mortgage Inc. continued to increase. Our business flourished while our competitors were closing doors and laying people off.

The stars get the business when it's tough to get, and when business gets good again, their market share automatically gets a boost. But this NEVER happens if you're hanging out with the Professional Doomsayer.

**Stay clear
of doom-saying.**

**You'll accomplish
more in a week than
the doomsayer does in
a month of moaning.**

NEVER COMPLAIN

Complaining is a learned skill. Well, maybe it's not a skill, but whatever it is, there are sure a lot of people around who can teach you how to do it. I never really got hooked up with one of those teachers. Maybe I've just been lucky.

Actually, **I was very lucky to have mentors in my industry who taught me how to understand customer needs and how to address those needs while instilling confidence.** I know one thing: The very worst way to secure a customer or build a team around yourself is to complain all the time.

Especially when I was in a more rigid corporate setting, I was amazed and frustrated to see my employees and colleagues in the mortgage business complain end-lessly about rates and fees and other ordinary aspects of our field. This constant complaining drained them of energy, brainpower, talent and money!

Be aware: the fellowship of the miserable will ALWAYS be around to teach you the intricacies of complaining. They have to. Without your cooperation they wouldn't have an audience.

Did you ever have a job in an environment where you were *persona non grata* if you didn't act miserable? My bet is that you have. And isn't it unpleasant to come into that kind of situation? If you *ain't* miserable going in, you're damn sure gonna be after spending time listening to your new bad-mouthing buddies.

I would tell my salespeople when I was in a more rigid corporate atmosphere: "You are paid a healthy commis-sion to generate business – you are not paid a healthy commission to sell the easiest thing there is in the world to sell. If that were the case, we would have people taking orders – not selling. The 'best' price shop is the 'best' price shop because they are not paying a healthy commission – that money is going into something else like advertising. You want a healthy commission? Then take the opportunity that you are being afforded and go make a sale."

Don't complain about the pricing of your products. Complain – excuse me, I mean, "make positive suggestions" – about procedures and systems and better ways to get things done. More times than not, creating efficiencies will overcome pricing issues.

- Are products being rolled out on time?

- How are we responding to the customer?

- Are our customer service evaluations laudatory, or do they indicate frustration on the part of the customer?

- Can we do our work faster and easier and with less paper?

These are the kinds of questions that should be asked in a firm striving to be a great customer service provider.

Put your synergy, energy, and thinking into these types of issues, rather than complaining, or you will drain yourself of your most precious commodity – your energy.

Think of your energy base as a **block of ice**. Once some of it melts it is gone! Mortgage support personnel, like underwriters and processors, the ones who do all the tough grunt work, have a shortened life span in the mortgage business when their energy melts like a block of ice. They get worn out and fussed at and frustrated so much with the pressures and complexities of the business, and one day they just can't do it anymore.

Every frustration turns up the heat that melts and melts and melts away at their block of ice. I am sure this is true of any support person in a financial service industry – a commodity broker's assistant or the person that gets the tough work done in an insurance office. Others call this burnout.

I am always careful to watch the energy supply on my personnel. If their ice is melting because they have to do senseless, repetitive things I get it resolved ASAP. **I don't let their ice melt – and the biggest melting agent known to man is complaining!**

Your energy can only melt ONE time, then it's gone!

> **The biggest cause
> of energy
> melt down
> is
> COMPLAINING!**

INTANGIBLE SALES–
THE PHYSICAL
DIFFERENCE

The general group of "intangible sales" includes selling products like mortgages, stocks, bonds, annuities, and insurance. I believe there is a major requirement to get these types of sales – they require **physical movement**. You must be able to get around to the companies and locales where you do business. **This will make a significant difference in the way you are accepted and appreciated by your external customer.** I can tell you this: most of your competition will not do it.

Recently, my stockbroker, who is a leading producer, has been learning this fact of life. He has been a top-ten type in his company for years, but he has just started getting out to see customers in the last three years. It has paid off dramatically. Not only does physically getting out of the office give you the chance to win new business (how many times have you had a stockbroker personally call on you?), but also it is a great way to reconnect and strengthen your relationships with existing customers.

To **distinguish your approach to customer service**, you must make the way you present yourself and your position different from the others in your profession.

If you are in intangible sales, **getting out to meet the customer will certainly distinguish you from others**. While my broker has learned the effectiveness of being physically dynamic in his job, his fellow brokers are sitting around the office crying about the market.

Of course that kind of behavior is not reserved only for stockbrokers. You should get a look at the mortgage industry. Loan reps sit on their fannies all day and at the end of the day, having written NO business, they complain and moan about the market being slow.

**If the market is slow get off your butt and
make it fast!**

Make seeing and presenting yourself to your customers a priority in your job behavior. The better you become at this, the more you will separate yourself from that part of your competition that does not do it. In selling intangible products, this is **the physical difference that will put you above the fray.** Providing this excellent customer service will get your story out in front of the competition.

People who are in intangible sales seem to have a resolve not to move; like there is a rule against it; like it's really not part of what they have to do to be successful. I don't know where this self-defeating attitude came from. Maybe it is an extension of the previous negative attitudes discussed in **"The Professional Doomsayer"** and **"Never Complain."**

Believe me your customer is less interested in your big fancy desk, up-to-date computer, or latest phone system and is much more interested in getting a personal visit from you.

**Take the time
to get out
of your office
and meet
your customers.**

Movement = Money!

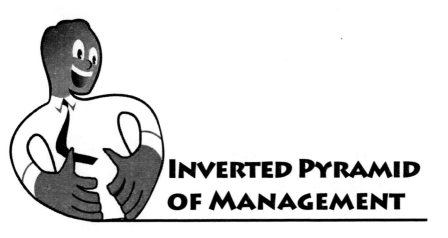

INVERTED PYRAMID OF MANAGEMENT

Being great at business requires a commitment from management – in support of personnel – that varies greatly from the traditional ways of doing things in most companies. I'm convinced that you must give people the opportunity to be great at their jobs.

People want to be great at their jobs!

I believe that to be a basic desire for just about any productive, driven person. I think the workplace today can be a de-motivating environment if a person continually feels that his or her talents are not being valued and used. It even seems to surpass de-motivation – to an unfortunate state where employees just give up.

47

Here is an example from my own experience:

A few years ago my mother injured her back and had to go to the emergency room. While I was waiting near my mother's room in the ER, an ambulance arrived and brought in a new patient. I admired the way the EMS attendant cared for this new patient and handled the situation in general.

After the patient was taken away, the attendant began to fold up and put back together the complicated roller/cot on which the patient was brought in. I commented to her, "That is quite a contraption – did you guys design that?" She then began to tell me everything that was wrong with the design, and how it could have been done better. "This should fold this way, so the patient has enough room... and this should go that way, etc., etc."

After her comments I said, "Didn't the manufacturer know that beforehand?" She replied, "No, because they just did it without asking us anything about what the patients' needs are. They never ask us. We're just peons."

Here's what you just read. Here's a caring employee who does her job well. She would have had positive impact on improving her company's equipment and it's ability to provide excellent service, if the company had a format in place to engage with their employees.

What has happened instead is that she has surrendered. It is less painful for her to surrender than to maintain her desire to be great at her job and be continually unfulfilled or disappointed. She has chosen to be the victim of *they*. It is a way for her to go about her job and not be the victim of her high expectations.

Why wouldn't her employer LISTEN to employees like her, or at least send them a questionnaire regarding the design of a new gurney, and what their ideas would be on how to make it great? Why do companies today not take advantage of their greatest asset – their employees?

Your job, as a leader or salesman or business-owner, is to make the workplace and the job satisfaction level of your employees/teammates as rewarding as possible. Actually, it is pretty easy to accomplish. All you have to do is let them use their talent and drive to be great at their jobs!

The opposite is not true – it is NOT their job to make your environment wonderful. It has taken me awhile to learn this lesson. The more you engage your employees, the more you will be rewarded. You'll know in a hurry if you've got the right people, because if they can't respond or thrive in this scenario, they are not capable of being fulfilled coworkers.

With the inverted pyramid form of management, the support team knows that their employer values their talents and abilities, and they will take a personal stake in promoting success in every situation that they can get their hands on.

The traditional pyramid (all ideas from the top down) model doesn't work – at least it doesn't give the level of success that separates your business from the crowd.

I have always had three commitments to my employees/ teammates:

1. That they are provided a business setting where they are supported to do the right thing. Always. Black and white when it comes to ethics and behavior.

2. That they are paid a premium to do their job better.

3. That they are provided with the tools necessary to be GREAT at their jobs.

Use inverted pyramid management.

Give employees what they most want –
A chance to be great at their jobs!

ONE
EXTRA CALL

Consider this scenario: *Let's say you are running a restaurant. You have a disgruntled customer. Everything has gone wrong. The salad had the wrong dressing. The baked potato was half raw. The steak was perfectly prepared but the steak knife had dried egg on it. The bill was wrong because your new computer system charged the customer twice for the wine.*

As the customer was leaving the restaurant, he tripped and banged his knee on the edge of the bar. After he paid the bill, you, the owner, ran after him and refunded his money. Only after all this happened did you find out that the customer was the restaurant critic for the major local newspaper.

Events like these are discouraging and mentally exhausting. They take a lot out of you and your team. They are stressful and aggravating. Of course, it is even easier to get aggravated in instances where the customer is truly unreasonable and out of line.

Sometimes we just fail to put ourselves in the customer's shoes. We can become a little thin-skinned when the customer wants a problem resolved and gets a little pushy.

Keep in mind that today's advertising tells customers how important they are, and that the customer's satisfaction is the mission of the company doing the advertising. So, in today's business environment, the customer expects – even demands – a lot.

People look at things from their own points of view. It is **easy to feel that we've done enough** for an irritating customer; that we have already exceeded normal helpfulness; and that nothing more needs to be done. Or, that if we did anything more, we would be humbling ourselves too much. Why, it would be a violation of our dignity!

This attitude of having done enough is a dangerous way to look at things, because all you have to go by is your own perspective. You are seeing things from the inside out and not from the customer's point of view.

In those cases where the customer has, in your opinion, worn you out with demands to fix a problem, here's something to try. In such situations, **try to get in the last helpful word**. In other words, make one extra call.

I realize you may *think* you have pleaded and coddled and refunded and done all the things that have put you over the limit of reasonable helpfulness, but the lethal question is "what if you haven't?"

What if all the time and effort you have put into this brouhaha was "one extra call" short of pleasing the customer? What if by one call you just missed creating an unofficial ambassador of goodwill for your company? This is what your disgruntled customer **can be** converted into if you handle the situation correctly. (More about this later in the *Psychology of Customer Service Evaluations.*)

Call the irritated customer one more time even after you think you have won the Nobel Prize for helpfulness.

You have extended a lot of time and effort, and sometimes expense, to win the customer back – **wouldn't it be a shame if you were just one call short from succeeding?** How awful. You won all the regular season and playoff games and lost the Super Bowl.

**Don't fall short
of pleasing
the customer.**

**Make ONE
extra call.**

VOICE MAIL

A lot of people hate voice mail, except those who use it to hide. Almost all companies have it nowadays. My company, Paul Karem Mortgage had NO voice mail during office hours. This distinguished us from our competitors, and we found that it actually was a positive experience, although it took a little work.

Since you and your company probably do use voice mail, the important thing is that you use it effectively. You handle it one way for the external customer and a different way for the internal customer (members of your team and company).

Paul's helpful hints for using voice mail:

For the external customer you retrieve and **respond to your calls continually** — just because you emptied your voice mail at 11:03 doesn't mean that you don't have a great sales opportunity waiting on your voice mail at 11:06. Just as importantly, your continual retrieving of messages will insure that you have an immediate reading on any damage control with problem situations or disgruntled customers.

When I had a luncheon with my sales team, it drove me nuts when they sat through the luncheon without ever checking their cellular voice mail messages. Personally, I feel like I've dropped the ball if someone calls me at 12:02, and I do not retrieve the message until I have finished my lunch at 1:15.

Maybe I'm a little obsessive, but I just don't think the customer gives a damn if I just checked my voice mail three minutes before he or she called. Some professionals think this gives them a built-in excuse for their late responses – you've heard this one a million times: "I just checked my messages before lunch." I say, if you want to be responsive to your customers – you have to check messages continually.

For the internal customer use the system as it is named – voice mail. That's voice mail, not voice phone tag. If you have a message to deliver or you want to relay information to a member of your team, give them all the information just as if you were sending them a letter in the mail. Tell the **whole story** so they can respond in the same fashion and resolve the issue.

Don't just leave your name and number. Don't leave an uninformative message and wait for them to call back... so you can call them back...so they can call you back... so you can call them back... so they can call you back. Haven't you been through that nonsense enough times? Give the contacted person all the necessary information, and let them respond or handle the situation from that point on. Avoid this phone tag. Don't keep the messaging going back and forth.

Handle these two groups, external and internal customers, differently. Give the external customer a fast response and give the internal customer the whole story. The external customer, particularly in this day and age of rapid exchanges of information, wants a personal response fast.

> **Voice mail –**
> **Don't use it to hide.**
>
> **Respond**
> **quickly and CONTINUALLY**
> **to external customers.**
>
> **Tell the *whole story***
> **to your internal customer –**
> **your team members.**

MAKE SURE THEY KNOW YOU WERE THERE

A core strategy for a mortgage loan originator is to call on, and seek referrals from, realtors. Making these calls myself, I found out two very important things about dealing with customers at their places of business. These two approaches have helped me grow my business and provide excellent customer service. The techniques are applicable in other markets and may help you in your business.

I made sure that I not only called on realtors in person, **_Intangible Sales – The Physical Difference_**, but whenever they referred a loan to me, I made sure I took the mortgage application into the realtor's office. Most of my competition either refused to do this, because they saw it as unprofessional, or wanted to stay planted in their own offices.

To be honest, the reason I did this initially was because I was trying to kill two birds with one stone. I was trying to write some business and visit the office on a sales call at the same time. I found this practice to be a real maximization of my time, efficiency, and effectiveness.

First and foremost, you are able to gain acceptance from your customer's colleagues when they see their cohort – especially if it's the office star or top-producer – dealing with you! You and the office star are sending a message that **the best is dealing with the best.**

This is one great reason to always have target projects aimed at key people—it's a real shortcut to getting the attention of other potential clients as well as a way to stand out from the competition.

The other benefit from this "get out and meet" technique was that I was able to take advantage of the opportunity to show the other realtors that I had been in their camp. I left business cards, loan rate sheets, company literature, and brochures and anything else I could think of all over the place, every time. I mean I really left a trail. They knew I had been there. I am not saying I disrespected someone's workplace, but they knew I had traveled through. This method of self-advertising became very valuable.

One other thought: Whenever I took a loan application into the realtor's office, I always welcomed the realtor into the loan application interview, with the blessing of the borrower. This used to be standard practice but with the advent of Internet mortgage applications has become rare.

Moreover, I ALWAYS used this time to give the realtor a sincere compliment in front of the borrower. You can believe me when I tell you that this was one of the most valuable sales tools in my career for bonding with the realtor. They loved and appreciated the kind, unsolicited words. "This is a very well written contract." Or, "You will love living in this part of town." These are the kinds of remarks that will go a long way toward improving your business relationships.

If you want to be a superstar of customer service and promote your business at the same time, develop a sense of the value of a subtle, sincere and well-placed compliment.

Don't be reluctant to get out of your own office to make a customer service/sales call.

And make sure everybody in the office you visit knows you were there.

**Get out of your office –
make customer service/sales calls.**

**Make sure everybody
knows you were there!**

"I DON'T DO THAT STUFF."

When I went into business for myself, I was overwhelmed by the minutia with which a self-employed businessperson is faced in this whiz-bang age of technology.

Immediately, I was hit with an onslaught of decisions to make regarding things I didn't really know much about. Computers, modems, DSL lines, file backup, phone forwarding, software selections, phone and computer system compatibility, a paperless vs. a traditional office, firewalls, ganibulators and whatamacallits and gibwopplers. I thought I was starting my own mortgage business—I didn't know I was constructing a wing of Cape Kennedy!

Since I really didn't know what I was doing, I chose the standard and most practiced strategy: I played the role of the village idiot, with the fashionable and acceptable twist that technophobes use, saying,
"I don't do that stuff" or "I don't know that stuff."

This is the firewall that we build around ourselves when we have self-doubt or an attack of laziness. I can tell you from experience that when you take this tack you are setting yourself up for disaster, frustration and looking ridiculous in front of your employees.

"Just get a computer guy in here" was my initial method of solving my troubles. It was just the start of my journey through five computer support people that I didn't jibe with until I got to the right one. Much of this was a massive waste of time and energy that could have been spent making sales calls and managing my business.

The lesson I learned was this: Saying, "I don't know that stuff" or "I don't do that stuff" in this day and time is EXACTLY EQUAL to saying "I don't know how to read" or "I can't spell." **If you don't know THAT STUFF then you better find out real fast.** It took me three years to get the right phone vendor, system software, computer supplier and support person.

If had I put in just a little more effort – I'm not talking about obtaining a master's degree in computers – I would have saved myself thousand of dollars, many frustrating hours, and the delightful experience of making a fool out of myself in front of my employees with childish temper tantrums.

After the millionth go-round with these issues, I resolved that I was finally going to get it right. This decision got its impetus from a caring employee who had the guts to set me straight.

As I stumbled through these self-inflicted mishaps, I frequently made the loud proclamation to the office – and anyone else who was willing to listen, "I'll be glad when I don't have to deal with this anymore and get transferred back to the Sales Division!" I thought I was being *cute*. What I did not know was just how onerous this behavior was in terms of the message it was sending to my fellow employees, my team-mates. I'm speaking of the lack of leadership and poor example that this behavior was giving to the people that run MY businesses and do the work that puts food on our families' tables.

Because our mortgage operation was so successful, we were able to operate a separate title company that essentially closed the majority of the loans issued by Paul Karem Mortgage. A former employee of the mortgage company, Debra Bates, operated the title company. Like our entire team she was talented, unusually bright, and understood **above the fray behavior and thinking**.

It was Debra who reprimanded me for the obnoxious and frequent fits about being "transferred back to the sales department." I heard her out and took the advice she was willing to give me. You will **NEVER** find a better group to learn from than caring employees. After my behavior adjustment I wrote Debra a long and appreciative letter, excerpted here:

One of the true pleasures in owning a business is interaction with motivated, skilled employees. The most gratifying reward is the chance to LEARN from your employees. I don't think a lot of employers realize this, and I base that on the people I have worked with/for previously.

Some were charismatic, passionate leaders who would take in what one had to say and react to the feedback in an energized and thoughtful manner. Some didn't care what you had to say and were more concerned about getting to their manicure appointments on time. I always knew which of these two categories you had to be in to be a successful employer.

The first thing I learned from you was that there was a value in my messages/mailouts, etc. I never grasped the value of my written anecdotes until you said to me one day, "...no one else tells people these things." It hit me in the head like a ball bat. In all my time and years of doing this stuff I had never had an employee make a remark like that to me. You taught me something about myself. The only thing I ever got from another employee along these lines was a whimsical smile or laugh about something I had written. You showed me that it had real value.

The next thing you taught me was that no team wants to hear their leader be a crybaby. When I was crybabying around about being "transferred back to the sales department" you let me know in a subtle way that it was not becoming of me to act that way. That I was above that. That you, your teammates and I deserved better. Additionally, you gave me a thought for a new part of my book. A chapter entitled "I don't do that stuff." That chapter is addressed to the leaders/managers who are in the mode that I was in when I made those remarks. Kind of like the guy who likes to say "I don't do that computer stuff – I'm too old so I let someone else take care of it." I see that to be what it is – a lazy cop out.

You MUST embrace and master all aspects of your business. When this hit me, I determined to get all the IT issues solid within my company. The reason they weren't until now was ME! I fixed that by learning about this stuff, seeking out and recruiting the right vendors and asking them the tough questions, and getting what my employees and I deserved. I saw that I had to make a change in this area, and you are the reason.

Remember, the first of the three steps in this book on how to serve and manage your internal and external customers is about **how to manage yourself**. You CANNOT accomplish the next two steps unless you can master the first one. **The most pathological way to fall short of this first step is to show bad example and poor leadership by saying: *"I don't do that stuff."***

Be a leader, not a crybaby.

PART THREE:

BUILDING A TEAM

You can't do Part Three correctly –
build a great customer service team –

If you haven't learned to do Part Two correctly –
manage yourself.

INSIDE-OUT
SELLING

A successful sales or customer service operation functions as an inside-out sales unit. This is the core concept of this entire section on team building and is central to creating great customer service. An inside-out sales organization is one that engages the customer with great internal synergy. An outside-in sales organization is one in which the customer dictates and demands and the internal operation reacts to the dictates, demands and complaints.

Let me show how this works with an example from my own industry. In the mortgage business there is nothing more aggravating to the external customer – the borrower – than being nit-picked by the lender for more and more information.

As a borrower, you have probably experienced this aggravation at some point—a lot of folks have. The bank first tells you everything looks good on your loan application, then, five days later they must have a copy of your bank statement. Five days after that they want a copy of your divorce proceedings – and the property settlement. Five days after that they want your last 12 income vouchers, and so it continues ad nauseam.

Finally the customer raises a fit, and the lender backs off a little bit, and the deal finally gets done. It happens in our industry continually. That is outside-in selling. The loan officer is not connected to the loan processor, and the loan processor is not connected to the underwriter, and the underwriter is not connected to the closer. Just like a restaurant where the hostess is fighting with the waitress, and the waitress is fighting with the chef, and the bartender has a beef with the manager so the customers get rotten service.

Remember an outside-in sales organization is one in which the customer demands and the internal operation reacts to the demands – and customer complaints. In the instance above, the mortgage company was not working as a harmonious team. No one was willing to take ownership of facilitating the customer's loan efficiently. Finally, the external customer made a complaint and the complaint got passed along so a loan was processed, but a lot of good will with the customer was lost. Not only did no one take responsibility for causing the problem, but even worse—THE GROUP AS A WHOLE DID NOT TAKE OWNERSHIP.

From 1989 to 1994, AmSouth mortgage was a great

customer service organization and a leader in inside-out selling. The company recognized the industry's run-of-the-mill faux pas, like the one described above, and did something about it.

AmSouth developed a plan for processing mortgage loans called the "first time approval system," an advance plan for pleasing the customer. Each member of the processing chain was rewarded for having a high percentage of "first time approvals." In other words, approving the loan the first time around with no extra "gets" from the external customer.

Think about how smart that is. It puts everyone in a position of responsibility for having a successful transaction with the external customer. The salesman or loan officer has to get the proper documentation at the beginning. The processor has to have a complete file when it is submitted to the underwriter. The underwriter can't be a nitpicker or bully with the file and must approve it the first time around as simply and cleanly as possible.

Everyone has the same mission. The mandate is excellence. Everybody has got to become a little better at their job – a little better at anticipating the problems down the line and taking care of them as soon as possible – and not letting a problem pass to the next person.

Internal turmoil and challenges must be directly addressed and resolved before you are ready for the external customer. You don't have to do it this way – you can settle for the mediocre manner that is becoming the order of the day in American business. God knows, a lot of businesses run without customer service excellence and exist.

I bought my mother a supplemental medical insurance policy to tie in with her Medicare. After she was enrolled I received a letter from the insurance provider that stated: "Welcome to XXXX Insurance, please note the information on your enrollment card. If there is any incorrect information please call customer service at 1-800-blah-blah. Our customer service representatives are standing by ready to help."

Sure enough, my mother's Medicare number was incorrect on the form – off by one digit – so I called their 800 number. It should have been so easy. Such a simple thing to get fixed, off by one digit...one number...ONE!

Over the next two weeks, I tried to call the 800 number twelve times. I tried on Saturday late, Sunday early, and every other time the recording told me I had a better chance of access. I punched my way through phone trees – if you wish to return to the main menu press 9 – talked to recordings and even to some *real* people and was continually told access was unavailable at that time. All this to change one digit. This minor fix simply could not be accomplished! I turned the project over to one of my brothers.

Moral of the story—this is a successful insurance company that makes money and carries a well-performing stock, but why do it this way? Why make enemies with your customers when you can use every interaction to build loyalty?

Your chance for trend-setting success is going to be limited if you find that you have disarray within your own walls in the form of differing philosophies, work habits, attitudes toward courtesy, phone-behaviors, and especially varying levels of knowledge and buy-in to your company's mission.

Spend the time and effort that is required in your particular situation to accomplish solidarity and buy-in. You will have a better mousetrap that will stand the test of time. Don't forget—all this is moot if you don't have what we talked about in Part Two—self-management.

> **Sell inside first.**
> **Then the**
> **ENTIRE operation**
> **will win**
> **the outside customer.**

TELL THE
SAME MESSAGE

Each member of your team should have the exact same impression of the important items that relate to your business. Each teammate should be on the same page in a number of important areas. A few of these are:

NUMBER 1   **What business are you in?** This sounds pretty basic. But, read the examples below and then give some thought to answering this question for yourself. It could be crucial to your success.

I have a close friend in Louisville named Tim Meagher who is very successful in the trucking business. He owns and operates three terminals in three different cities. The transport business is an extremely competitive industry, and the margins are very tight. Tim is constantly reminding his staff "we are not in the trucking business – we are in the money-making business."

Think about how smart that is. It is a constant reminder to his teammates not to get caught up in the competitive trap when they are trying to secure a contract. It means that the company will stand behind them if they lose a deal because there just was not enough profit in it. That is reassuring and gives the employee the means to act confidently. Also, it is a way for teammates to be clear on their mission when they are trying to pursue business. A directive like this is a constant reminder of what is really important in one's work setting.

I stole Tim's idea and changed his saying to something that worked well for us in our business. My slogan to my teammates was "we are not in the mortgage business – we are in the realtor service business." This is what we really did. The salespeople and I traveled around all day (see *Intangible Sales*) calling on real estate companies to tell them about our products and services. Visiting realtors is one of the main sources of sales referrals in the mortgage business. Therefore it is critical for the support staff to know how key it is for the realtor to be well informed and treated with customer service excellence when a deal is referred. Realtor service was our real business.

NUMBER 2 **Do it the same way.** Make sure that all the personnel who talk to external customers do it the same way. This means that your receptionist, support personnel, salespeople, closer, etc.

quote rates and fees and services in the same manner. Believe me, achieving this takes practice and communication with your team. Right now, they all think they are on the same page, but they are not. When you present this concept, you will hear a surprised, "oh yeah," many times as they discover how they can more consistently mirror the presentation of your product.

My friend, Tim Coury, owns – in my and many other's estimation – the best restaurant in Louisville, Porcini. One rule he has is that a server can NEVER answer a request from a customer with, "Who is your waiter?" or "I'll tell your waiter." The server is instructed to take the request and give it to the waiter. The point of this directive is – don't quiz or aggravate the external customer. This instruction is given to all his personnel so new employees get the courteous feel and style of his restaurant – and so they can all do it the same way.

NUMBER 3 **Have a mission.** Write a mission statement for your group/division/company. *Everyone* in the group needs to participate in writing the mission statement. Be sure to get some part of the statement from everybody who is involved so there is buy in.

Make sure you reach absolute agreement on what the mission is before you post it in the office. You might even want to consider putting it in a place where the external customer can view it, if this is appropriate for your industry.

The three keys to telling the same message:

1. What business are you in?
2. Do it the same way.
3. Have a mission.

All Do
All Things

If you want to be unusually successful in your career, **above the fray**, you must maximize the utilization of your two biggest resources: time, and the talented people you have around you. Optimizing these resources effectively gives you the power to set your company apart from the competition.

To take the first step in this process, you have to convince your staff to develop the mind-set that they are willing and able to do more than just one job or task. I call this approach, "All Do All Things." As a manager, encouraging this can be quite a challenge. You may well encounter resistance. Doing one job one way maintains a comfort level for many of your team. They feel threatened when asked to act outside of their well-defined territory.

In the mortgage business, it is generally accepted that the processor hates to do what the originator is "supposed" to do, the originator hates to do what the processor is "supposed" to do, the closer won't do what the underwriter is "supposed" to do, and they each have a moat built around their desks. Is it like that in your business or are you synergized and **treating each other as customers?**

Based on my own experience, I am going to give you some ideas that will help you to encourage your staff to work more cooperatively. Putting these concepts into practice, you will help your team members to develop a more productive mindset.

Basically there are only two types of tasks: **selling and support**. In a lot of management settings the saying goes, "never the twain shall meet." However, for your organization to be great, you have got to make the line between the sales and support groups to disappear. Optimally, these two functions should function seamlessly.

This important step in team development is most effective if your team is already on message, knows what the real business of the company is, and has bought into the company's mission. In other words, you will now be building on the foundation of what I suggested in the previous chapter, *Tell the Same Message*.

To begin the process of integrating the selling and support functions in your office, begin with the basics. First, make it a part of everyone's job description that each support person is to take on the mindset of

– and perform as – a sales person, and that every sales person is to take on the mindset of – and function as – a support person. Make sure that the people you employ accept this integrated approach with a helpful and willing attitude. If they do not – you might have the wrong people.

To clarify how this works in a real office setting, here are some actual examples of "All Do All Things" in action:

• An insurance salesman gives certain authority and leeway to his administrative assistant or selected staff members to distribute certain sales-related information to existing and prospective clients.

• When a couple comes into a restaurant and asks for a specific table because it is a special occasion – their anniversary, the hostess makes the waitress aware of what's going on. Knowing this, the waitress makes sure the happy couple has an evening to remember. The couple appreciates the thoughtful service and they become regular customers.

If you think this sounds like too simple an example, and you are sure such things are done on a regular basis, you are sadly mistaken. Small sensitivities like this are sorely missing in service industries today.

• A saleswoman who is responsible for a certain account retrieves important documents from the fax machine and delivers them to the desk of the administrative assistant. Too simple? Too basic? Try it in your office and see how it improves time-sensitive customer service.

Do you see how important it is to develop this approach? Can you imagine your team synergized like this, and what this implementation could do to your productivity and bottom line?

What does setting up a synergistic, "All Do All Things" environment accomplish?

NUMBER 1 You build good will with the external customer. Your customers are comfortable and satisfied dealing with all of your people.

NUMBER 2 You maximize your own time because you are freed up to meet and engage new customers. Your team members are so effective that you don't personally have to hold the regular customer's hand at every turn. **You have turned every selling moment into two.**

NUMBER 3 You have set a rewarding expectation for the external customer—awareness that they have finally found a vendor that gives them fast, dependable, considerate service.

When "All Do All Things", your **internal teamwork** provides the customer a sense that you are *above the fray.* After getting a taste of this kind of service from you, your customers will require more from your competitors – **and in the vast majority of cases they will not receive it.**

NUMBER 4 With your synergistic team in place, you will have created an extension of your sales self that will function seamlessly all day, everyday.

NUMBER 5 You are creating opportunities for multiple sales in the place and time-span usually needed for one.

> **Manage your company**
> **so that "All Do All Things"!**
>
> **Develop unparalleled service**
> **– and loyalty**
> **in your customers!**

DEALING WITH
THE BEAN-COUNTER
AND THE TECHNICIAN

If you are in sales you have to deal with a bean-counter and/or a compliance technician somewhere along the way in your business.

This is a classic conflict in the American business setting, for all the wrong reasons. Most of those wrong reasons have to do with not knowing enough about the other guy's job or the other guy's responsibilities.

Very few companies are willing to do what AmSouth Mortgage Company (a company where I once worked and learned a great deal) did in developing an internal customer service mandate that extended to ALL areas of the operation. In essence this mandate **forced** each member of the team to know a little bit more, and have a little more regard for, the other person's job.

Absent this kind of leadership, you have to take it upon yourself to develop the synergy that is only found in the greatest companies. In more ordinary circumstances, it is likely that you are going to have to develop a trusting and respectful relationship with your team by using your own head and talents. This should be your first goal – to win the respect of your associates, not to overpower or intimidate or out-argue.

Wouldn't it be a more pleasant world if everybody in an office was obligated to do another person's job for six weeks or so?

Let's first look at an example from the industry where I have the most experience, the mortgage loan industry. In this industry, the loan originator brings in loans and the underwriter approves or denies the loans.

In a non-communicative setting, the salesman will think the underwriter is a nitpicker and deal-killer, and the underwriter thinks the salesman is an obnoxious egomaniac that is only about money, money, money and making a big commission. If they only knew that each one's job security is totally dependent on the other's skill and expertise, it would be a great revelation for them. If those two traded jobs for six weeks, they would either get out of the business and go into ditch-digging, or have a greater understanding of the bigger picture.

Here's another example: In a restaurant you have a hostess, a waitress and a chef. A couple comes into the restaurant and rejects the table where the hostess offers to seat them. They demand a booth in a different area. The hostess responds appropriately and seats them in their requested spot.

Meanwhile, there are sub-plots developing all over the place. Frances, the waitress, wants them to sit at the initially recommended table because that table is in her area; she has waited on them before and has gotten a good tip.

However, seated in their requested booth, they now have Frank for a waiter. He is unhappy about this because he is waiting on a gorgeous single-girl named Violet at another table. Serving this couple will take time away from his mission of romancing Violet.

Not only that, but the couple are fussy about their steak orders, and so Frank has to take their under-cooked steaks back to Chef Hans with whom Frank does not get along. Hans is going to go off when finicky Frank returns with the incorrectly prepared steak and announces it to the entire kitchen.

The whole restaurant is in disarray because the staff is concentrating on everything except the customer. Frances wants a big tip. Frank wants to make time with a cute customer, and the chef wants to win an award in *Chef Monthly*.

Nobody is thinking about the customer, who is the key to all of their goals! If all the customers' needs are attended to, Frances will experience a wealth of good tippers. If all the staff concentrates on the customer,

Frank will be in a successful setting and just might feel confident enough to court the Violets of the world away from his job at the restaurant! If the chef begins to listen to the wait staff's customer preferences, mistakes like under-cooked steaks are less likely to happen; the restaurant will be more successful; and the chef will be able to hire an assistant to take some of the pressure off, so he can prepare orders to the diner's delight. When they focus on individual instead of shared goals, the hostess gets in the waitress's way, and the waiter gets in the chef's way. **They don't know it but they're blocking their OWN way – to success.**

This restaurant example can be applied to any institutional setting. In every organization there is either a shared circle of success or a whirlwind of confused goals that creates a vortex of failure.

The whole circle of success starts, collectively and individually, when the larger mission is successful. That is the difference between teams that win Super Bowls and the other NFL teams that lose most of their games. Believe me, they all have plenty of talent.

Your individual goals will come to fruition when you **win over your entire internal team** – including the folks from that weird division down the hall that always gets in the way.

> **Lead your team
> to focus on the customer,
> live the mission, and
> respect everyone's
> contribution to the work.**
>
> **Each will benefit
> from the company's
> success.**

I CAN'T GO IN
THE KITCHEN

Recently I was out having lunch with a friend, and he inquired with our waiter about the status of his overdue sandwich order. The waiter's response was; "I think it's ready but waiters can't go into the kitchen." End of conversation. Done. Left hanging. Starving with no hope of getting food – or even an explanation.

This is an example of a waiter, but it could have been any customer service provider, who was prevented from being good at his job because of some insane "inside" rule that he did not have enough pride to challenge.

To stay with the restaurant analogy: If you have a customer who needs an answer from the kitchen, but according to management rules the kitchen is off limits, you have got to find another way of figuring out what is going on in there.

This applies to ALL businesses – not just the restaurant business. This section could easily have been titled, *I Can't Go In The Accounting Department* or *I Can't Call The Underwriters After 3:00 PM*. You simply cannot deliver such a pathetic message to your customer! You can't state your company's equivalent of, *"I can't go in the kitchen"* and expect to have satisfied customers.

Certainly, I'm not suggesting that you ignore all company rules, but there has **got** to be a better way to deliver a logical, courteous message to your customer. There has **got** to be a better way to respond to the requests of customers who are trying to spend their money with your establishment.

So what do you do when management has left you in what seems like an uncompromising position? You use your God-given talents to find some way to answer the customer's request. You might wonder at this point – "what *could* the poor waiter have done?"

Here are two schools of thought:

Option 1: Even if you, the waiter, "can't go in the kitchen", somebody else must have access. Otherwise how does the food get in and out of there? Since somebody goes in the kitchen, doesn't it make sense to know, or find out who that person is, in the event an instance like this comes up? That way you can get the present status of the customer's sandwich *from the guy who is allowed in the kitchen* and deliver the message to the customer without making yourself, and the entire operation, look foolish.

Option 2: Present this problem to management when the timing is right. The "right timing" might mean when the situation is taking place, and therefore require some sense of urgency. Or, it could mean you should talk about it after the fact, when you and the manager can sit down and discuss the dilemma you were faced with calmly and sensibly.

To analyze this internal communication issue from the level of management, let's return to the restaurant model: If this restaurant had a customer service mandate in place, the issue would resolve itself quickly. You can be sure that if the manager were put in the position of having to tell a customer that he, himself, didn't know the status of the customer's sandwich because he "couldn't go in the kitchen", the policy would be changed quickly.

If you manage yourself correctly, then you are prepared to effectively manage and lead your internal team. If you focus on the customer, you will not have rules like not letting the waiter "go in the kitchen."

When you find that you have made some ineffective rules, which will occasionally happen, then you must have the protocols in place to deal with them. Have a system in place to periodically monitor the effectiveness of all rules and regulations in order to select the ones that must be changed or eliminated. Such evaluation and tweaking can occur on an ongoing basis and will strengthen your business.

Your company will now have in place a system that constantly reviews procedures and seeks out suggestions on how to do things better. If you embrace this management style, your employees will feel respected and empowered. They will not be wasting time gossiping with one another or – even worse – with external customers about company rules and shortcomings. Anyone who sees a problem and has an idea about how to improve things can feel free to bring it to management. What a great way to use the talents of all the people involved in your business and at the same time reap the benefit of building and improving your business.

There is a powerful strength in **treating your internal team like customers**. You **never** leave someone in the lurch with an awkward or embarrassing way of handling a task. The embarrassing or awkward task should be left to management.

Let me put that another way – a way that stems from the core concepts of this book. **Management should RUN to the embarrassing or awkward task!** When you do this you demonstrate clearly your willingness to help the external customer and to set an example for your team! Additionally, you show your willingness to help your internal teammate – **AND THAT WILL COME BACK TO YOU IN SPADES!**

You CAN'T put
your teammates
in the position
of saying
to the customer,

"I can't get you the information
you need.
I can't go in the kitchen!"

INTERNAL SQUABBLES

Those of you who are managers are familiar with internal squabbles. I am referring to the in-house fussing that drives managers, or anyone who has a sense of "teamwork" crazy.

These disturbances are usually the work of the same people, over and over again. I am talking about the difficult types with whom you have to carefully measure and cautiously deliver every message.

There are, however, those other wonderful people who are so eager to please that they respond quickly to every request. They have a spirit of helpfulness and an earnest desire to improve not only their performance but to promote the success of the entire workplace.

The first group I liken to spoiled French Poodles. The second are the Golden Retrievers. (All deference and respect to French Poodle fans and owners).

In the office or corporate environment, the Poodle will not go past a barrier. As a manager, your relationship with Poodles never changes. Neither do the relationships they maintain with every other member of your team. Do you know an example of this type of employee?

On the other hand, The Golden Retrievers breeze past barriers with a smile and keep on retrieving. Their happiness comes from helping.

Golden Retrievers will help anybody, anytime. Above all, you don't have to measure words, even when the request is a bit difficult. Do you know of any examples of Goldens? Sure you do. We can recall the Goldens quickly because no one EVER forgets this kind of employee/teammate.

Isn't it ironic that the touchy Poodle is the one who is forgotten the soonest? In spite of the Poodles' efforts to put themselves on a pedestal, the helpful Golden is the one who stays in everyone's mind for a long time.

The trick, of course, is to get the Poodle to become a Golden Retriever. Guess what? There's only one way to do it – quick and fast.

In my experience, turning a Poodle into a Golden Retriever cannot be done over an extended period of time. It's a huge energy drain for all involved. To be successful, you have to give the Poodle a **quick, straight-forward,** and **direct evaluation** of their mannerisms in an enlightening manner. I have had success getting Poodles to change their behavior using role-play!

Role-play can be amazingly effective in getting through to a troubling employee, especially if this is done with other members of the team. The problem or challenge is timing. You have got to pick a time, or even a new setting, where you have the best chance of success.

One setting that has worked for me is an informal dinner or lunch with my team. The group is relaxed and has its guard down a bit. No one feels threatened and the atmosphere is pleasant. Sometimes I have used this setting to engage in role-play to make a point, and I have had really good luck with it.

Let me share this example of effective role-play that translated into my personal improvement:

> *Once I was having dinner with my staff. There was an issue hanging in the air that they wanted to tell me about but were hesitant to do so. After a few glasses of wine and a nice meal, the group felt relaxed and settled into some degree of informality. When we began a discussion about things we could all improve on, they responded in concert, "Paul you have got to take more detailed loan applications!"*
>
> *What they were revealing was that, in my haste – which has always been a problem for me – I was leaving important information off loan*

applications. These omissions of mine were making their jobs much harder. My associates were being left with the irritating task of going back to the borrower and asking for more information – a bad violation of our lofty customer service code.

When I questioned the validity of their criticism, the group went into an enlightening "play."

The group humorously dramatized what it was like to get an incomplete loan application from me! One of the more talented members of the group played the role of Paul, and I got a revelation – a real taste – of something that I needed to do differently and quick. It was funny as hell, but I got the point.

In this case, **role-play effectively cut through all our defenses and resulted in a very improved outcome**. This, of course, is just one way to proceed.

WARNING! Use an approach that you personally feel comfortable with – that reflects your style. This is a scenario that can go totally wrong if not done correctly and carefully.

If you still have not gotten through to the Poodle then go to Plan B.

Plan B involves having a direct talk while looking each other in the eye. Use this talk to **set an ultimatum**, and a good thing will happen. The Poodle will either tell you to kiss off or will finally get the point. Either way you win.

The pain of this exercise will be outweighed by the results 50 fold. I promise. I had a Poodle that simply could NOT stop crying. Every time something challenging or difficult or out of the norm came up, she started crying and it drove the team insane. Complaints came to me continually about Christie's (not her real name) behavior.

After we had our face-to-face ultimatum talk, she went on a typical crying jag. This time I did the following: I cut an ad out of the newspaper for the exact same job she had with us that was open at another mortgage company. I said to Christie, "Here is another job for you that pays about the same. You are well qualified, and I will give you an excellent reference." Christie never cried again. It was like someone had finally taken off her blinders. The whole office staff was thankful.

As an effective leader, when you are willing to take on the Poodles, your entire team benefits.

Encourage and treasure the Golden Retriever.

Confront the Poodle with role-play or ultimatum.

Good management prevents internal squabbles.

THE
VIDEO ROOM

You must strive to get yourself and your team to buy into an environment of **constant self-improvement**. That is a little touchy nowadays because everybody, somehow, has developed very thin skin, which is one of the main reasons this book needed to be written. It is difficult to speak frankly and directly to people about their shortcomings.

The ironic thing about this is that most people desire and embrace direct and frank constructive criticism once they have had a taste of the results. At the core, **we all want to be successful and dynamic at our vocations**.

More than money or accolades or titles or promotions or anything else that comes our way, what the human spirit desires most (in the business setting) is to be great at what one does for a living. All the trappings of success, like titles and promotions and, yes, money, are an after-the-fact effect of being great at your job.

If your people buy into Part Two, self-management, then you have the right group to embrace Part Three, becoming a team. However, to achieve a high level of teamwork, you have to be willing to speak frankly and candidly with each other.

Think of this experience as similar to the way an athlete goes about improving performance. **Michael Jordan**, for instance, **constantly** watched and critiqued himself by viewing game and practice videos (professional teams tape every practice). He opened himself up to **constant self-review and self-evaluation**. All this in order to pick up a competitive edge and improve his game.

I use Michael Jordan for my example because he is the greatest basketball player of all time, possibly the greatest athlete period, and even he did this self-evaluation constantly.

Can you imagine the power of a group of people that self-evaluates INDIVIDUALLY AND COLLECTIVELY? Can you imagine the force that can be created if a group commits itself to constant self-improvement and self-evaluation? Think of the benefits to a company – the improved performance levels – if individuals looked within for ways to improve and took critiques willingly from the people around them? It is a unique setting that promotes this kind of teamwork.

Realizing the benefits of self and group evaluation, why wouldn't a sales or business professional subscribe to the same mandate for excellence? I challenge you to conduct a forum in business today that is as effective and frank as those in which athletes participate when they watch the videos of a performance.

It is important to remember, that when these videos are viewed, it is in front of the entire team and coaching staff. This is an environment in which the players and coaches together confront the unvarnished truth that is revealed in the video footage. **All members of the team are evaluating each other**.

If you believe that "two heads are better than one" then how powerful do you think ten, fifteen or twenty are? All professional sports teams essentially have the same talent levels. Moreover, the professional athlete of today is incredibly gifted. Do you think the teams that win championships do it because they have the best players? You KNOW there is more to it than that!

They win because they have self-management of the highest caliber. They have evolved into a group who manage themselves as an unstoppable team.

Think of the characteristics of championship teams, like the New England Patriots. Do they have knuckle-heads on the team who beat their wives and get busted for drugs? Do they have players drawing attention to themselves? NO. They are a team of self-managed and synergistic professionals dedicated to a common cause. Believe me, there is an atmosphere in their locker room, absent of coaches and management that takes care of the individual that poorly self-manages.

In business today, there can be challenges that make this dynamic hard to create: Thin skin. Political correctness. An overly-paranoid human resource manager. Whatever. But, the results are so worthwhile that it's worth taking on these challenges. Can't we be as frank with each other, or as willing to hear frank statements from our associates, as an athlete in the video room? With the right leadership and attitudes, we can!

When I was with AmSouth, we had the most synergistic team with which I have ever been associated. We held a weekly meeting that was an open exchange of ideas unlike any I have encountered in a business setting since.

Weekly, one of our associates would say to me or another member of the group something like, "Evelyn, you did a good job on the Jones deal but you could have done better if..." When this kind of message was delivered it was also received in the **correct context** – one of teamwork and cooperation. Team members knew it was in their interest to embrace the suggestions and run with them.

There was no contention in the air. I don't know if we just had the right people for this approach, or if it was the example that was set for us. At any rate, it worked. It overpowered any urge to act like an overly-sensitive employee instead of a dedicated team player.

To give a down-to-earth example of helpful, constructive criticism, let's say you had a friend with an unfortunate habit or unpleasant behavior. Maybe he constantly cracked his knuckles, or she endlessly clicked her nails on the desk. It distracted and annoyed everyone, even alienated some clients, and was very unpleasant, but he or she was completely unaware of it. We've all experienced this, where everyone else is annoyed by the behavior **except the person who is engaged in it**. It might be **tough** to tell your friend about the distracting habit that bothered everybody but him. But, wouldn't you be doing him a big favor?

**Create an atmosphere
like the video room
so you can give one another
helpful advice
in an atmosphere
of constructive criticism.**

**Provide leadership
by your example.
Seek out advice
from your associates
on things
YOU need to improve!**

SHE DIDN'T
PICK IT UP

To have a great internal customer service platform, you must have a genuine respect for people. Sometimes that comes naturally and sometimes you have to work at it.

During one point in my career I was involved in moving an operation to another company. I got a signal early on that the merger was going to be a little bumpy. The first company was one that had invested a lot of time, energy and money into molding an entity with great internal customer service. Now, we were in the process of making a transition, moving our offices and personnel into the new setting.

One day I came into work early. One of the employees I was inheriting, a person who came from the group we were now joining, walked into the office entrance door ahead of me. She stopped at the door, stooped over to read the label of a package that someone had delivered, reared back up and walked into the office without the package.

When I got to the door, I examined the package. It was clear that it contained loan-related documents that an external customer had dropped off for a member of our team. The young lady ahead of me had not taken the time to pick the package up, walk an extra 12-15 feet, and drop it off at the intended person's desk.

My heart sank and my stomach got that queasy, Monday morning feeling for the first time in 5 years – the first time since I had started with AmSouth. Was I making a mountain out of a molehill? My gut told me I was not.

Maybe this seems like a non-event to you, but the most troubling thing to me was that I knew this apparent disregard for a fellow-employee would NEVER have happened at AmSouth.

As insignificant as it may seem to you, doing a little thing – like retrieving a package – goes a long way in building a team. Maybe the person for whom the package was intended was having an especially busy day. Maybe, just maybe, a small gesture like that might make things a little easier.

The **Poodle** had passed up the package and left it for the next **Retriever** to come along and handle the dirty work. However, in reality, **it's the fun work** –

not the dirty work – when you get to do something for someone else on your team.

> If you see something for Ed by the fax machine take it to him.

> If you see something for Edna by the copy machine take it over to her.

> If you see something at the front desk for Hortense take it to her.

> If you see some mail for Fred out in the lobby take it to Fred.

> If you see something for Julie by the front door take it inside to her.

This helpful approach might not sound like much, but it goes a long way to building a powerful team culture.

If you do something nice and courteous for someone, there is a great likelihood that they will do something nice and courteous for you. These actions jump-start the kind of synergy that is necessary for great internal customer service – **treating each other like customers**. And as simple as this strategy sounds, it creates another, very important, dynamic in your business environment. When someone new comes aboard, they quickly see what the rules are and how to respond to their new fellow employees.

> **Pick up and deliver the package!**
>
> **Jump-start great internal customer service –**
>
> **Treat each other like customers.**

EMPLOYEE CONTRACTS

Every year my employees and I wrote up contracts.

It was an exercise that eliminated a lot of confusion and wasted energy in the workplace.

This is how it works: I ask each person on my team to write a narrative about his or her job. They can make it as long or as short or as detailed or as generalized as they like. All I ask is that it be sincere, well thought-out, not rushed, and from the heart. It should include ideas about their goals, behavior on the job, and what they think is expected of them from the rest of the team. It can even incorporate open and candid commentary about other teammates, including me.

Most of the contracts end up being about two pages by the time I receive them. However, I have read some that were as long as ten pages and some as short as two paragraphs.

After the employee writes his or her job description or narrative, we review it together. Then we make both joint and individual comments on the content. Now here is the **real magic** of the exercise—we then form an agreement – a contract – on what that person's job is and how they are going to do it. Depending on the individual's situation or work history, the contract may be more detailed or less detailed. For instance, it may or may not delve into issues like mannerisms and body language.

When we have concluded the document, we both sign it just like a contract and it becomes our agreed-to working dictum. This is a great time to get stinky stuff out in the open and get rid of it for good. All it takes is straight talk and the right kind of people who are willing to listen to it.

My great friend, Jack Wheatley, who was a business mentor of mine, once told me, "How people perform on the job is 10% whom you hire and 90% how they are managed." At the time (twenty years ago) I believed this to the core and tried to use it to no avail. With all deference to my brilliant, late friend Jack, I don't think those percentages work in all cases. I think the correct percentages (for the 99% of managers who are not as gifted as Jack) are the exact opposite — it's 10% how you manage people and 90% whom you hire. Going through this contract exercise with your team members quickly clarifies whether you have hired the right people. (Look for more on this subject in **Adding to Your Team**.)

A former employee of mine, Carol Brightwell, who became a superstar with another lender, wrote remarkable contracts in our time together. In a contract that she wrote ten years ago, she touched on the following issues:

- Freeing the branch manager (me) of any internal duties so I could concentrate on sales

- Setting quotas for her personal production

- Expanding our "builder" business (Our company traditionally had not done much business with builders.)

- Coordinating her work time better with her baby-sitter

- Establishing a better closing system with our attorneys

- Attending a seminar to learn how to better control her emotions

- Help the branch win customer service awards (She wins one every year now.)

- Conducting more outside sales calls (Remember **The Physical Difference**?)

How can you go wrong with a person who so comprehensively embraces her job? All her contracts were this targeted and expansive. All I ever changed or added to Carol's contracts was the phrase "remember to enjoy your job. You can start by eliminating two of the above." I made her shorten her contract and remember to enjoy her job and not try to do everything for everybody in the operation.

Certainly I received some contract narratives that were less insightful, but in time those people "got it" as well.

One more very important step relates to the writing of contracts with your team. **It works both ways**. Yep, you have to write a contract as well. This states your commitment on how you will perform for your team. Most of my own contracts with my teams have included three points of emphasis:

 I will provide a work environment with the highest levels of ethics and morals.

 You will be given the tools to be great at your job.

 You will be paid at or above the market.

Establish a method for employee contracts.

Write your own contract. Give your teammates a chance to make changes or additions. And then sign it.

> **Utilize
> Employee Contracts.**
>
> **Write a
> contract yourself!**
>
> **Eliminate confusion
> and wasted energy
> in your workplace.**

ADDING TO
YOUR TEAM

If you have had the good fortune of proper self-management and the better fortune of building a team, you are on your way to creating something terrific.

Nevertheless – sooner or later – you will confront the issue of adding a new member to your team. Your dynamic, inspiring setting is going to attract a lot of people. Some of them will understand from the start what it takes to be great at their work and some will never get it.

A lot of people fall into the thinking that someone else is responsible for making them great in their chosen field. If you ask some of the players on the low-ranking NFL football teams, what it would take to make their team great, the answer would likely be, "We need a great head coach." Or, "We need to hire Bill Parcells."

Your challenge, when adding a member to your team, is to make sure the new addition is someone who **"gets it."**

In most business settings today, the attitudes and behaviors of the majority of the team quickly dictates the behavior of any new hires. In other words, if all the people that work at Eddie's Body Shop are snotty and snooty to the customers, the new hires will act exactly the same way. If the new hires attempt to be friendly and helpful, Eddie's dysfunctional team will soon treat them as outcasts.

On the other hand, **your great team will help to cast off bad hires**. A disgruntled worker functions poorly in a well-coordinated, synergistic setting. An effective leader never puts team members in the position of having to deal with a co-worker's negative behavior. So, here are some ways to filter out the unlikely prospects.

Follow these suggestions to select only those employees who have the best chance to "**get it**" and become productive members of your team:

 Verify that the candidate **wants** to be a member of the team. It is their job to win you over regarding their zeal and enthusiasm about your company. Not vice versa.

NUMBER 2

Make sure the candidate meets with other team members in addition to you. It is extremely effective to have key teammates meet a potential hire outside the business setting. And get their opinions!

NUMBER 3

Identify any control issues. Make sure the candidate is open to criticism, and that criticism is taken in the form of personal improvement.

NUMBER 4

It is prudent to use outside testing. There are excellent testing services providing personality-profile tests that are truly amazing. They can help you to analyze a candidate's probability for success in your industry by revealing personal attitudes and behaviors. The testing prevents the dreaded, unfortunate surprise a few days after you have hired someone.

NUMBER 5

Ask the candidate to recall a bad experience from which they gained valuable knowledge. You want somebody who learns from mistakes and is not afraid to pick up and go forward.

NUMBER 6

Contact the references. Hiring a new member for your team is a lot like buying a car. The amount of trouble you avoid down the line is in direct proportion to how much time and effort you are willing to put into the up-front inspection.

It is YOUR JOB
to *not*
saddle your team
with problem
co-workers.

OVERCOMING DISCREET CUSTOMER CONTEMPT

Do you recall the last chapter in Part One, where we looked at glaring examples of what I named, **discreet customer contempt**? We looked at many instances of supposed service providers who just couldn't be bothered to concentrate on the customer; instead they were obsessed with their own concerns. The examples included an inconsiderate and self-absorbed bank teller, an impolite, unfriendly waiter, a haughty auto mechanic, a forgetful mortgage guy, and, of course, the robotic customer service rep for the health insurance company.

We finally concluded that there were two likely causes for discreet customer contempt. I defined them as "the disconnect" and "thin-skinned self-righteousness."

We've already discussed many ways to overcome the disconnect in earlier chapters, but we still need some **ideas on how to overcome our thin-skinned self-righteousness**. This attitude poisons communication with customers today. It's important to remember that your business exists only if you have happy, satisfied customers. The boss **signs** the pay checks, but the customers **make** the checks good! You need delighted customers, who are not only pleased with your service, but also happy to spread the good word about your wonderful company!

Let's ponder these questions:

• Why do we consider it undignified to console and counsel an irate customer? What is it about being helpful to the irate customer that is so personally demeaning in this day and time?

It's not undignified or demeaning! You want people to recall all the help you were willing to provide. You need to see the irate customer as a professional challenge. You can actually begin to welcome the opportunity to win over even your most difficult customer.

• Why can't we see the person who can win over the irate customer for what they are – skilled service providers?

Accept the challenge when you are dealing with an irate customer. Go the extra mile. Stay calm and focused and find a way around, over or through the problem, whatever it is. Then, congratulate yourself for a real achievement.

• Why is providing great customer service to the irate customer so misunderstood as something humbling? Why do we hear the tired old adage "that's like kissing someone's behind! I don't kiss anyone's behind!" This thinking is wrong headed and unproductive.

If you want success, you need to begin to see this for what it really is – giving the customer what they want. It is not demeaning to give good service! In addition, we should feel good about the professionalism involved. It is **NOT** a humbling experience if we manage ourselves correctly and feel good about ourselves—it is a skill and a service.

Stay *above the fray* and use these methods to get rid of Discreet Customer Contempt:

NUMBER 1	**DROP** the thin-skinned, self-righteousness.
NUMBER 2	**EMBRACE** the customer. It's okay. It doesn't make you a lackey. If you think you are a lackey it is due to a bigger problem—NOT the complaints of the customer.
NUMBER 3	**DON'T** be like the customer service representatives you run into all the time who address you with a frown on their faces, or the service provider who has you on hold for forty-five minutes.

Stand *above the fray*
by providing
GREAT service...
NOT by protecting
your sensitivities.

How to Get Your Point Across

In 1967, I had the privilege of being recruited to play football for the University of Alabama. Alabama's coach, of course, was the great **Paul "Bear" Bryant** – the single most charismatic man I have ever encountered.

At the time of my recruiting trip, the Alabama team was ranked number two in the country and was playing South Carolina – which was a long way from being the respectable opponent it is today. After a lackluster first half, Alabama was slightly ahead. At the time this was a bit of an embarrassment for Alabama's football powerhouse. Especially since they were playing what was then a mediocre team.

As the squads ran to their respective locker rooms for halftime discussions with their coaches, my heart and head were full of anticipation and enthusiasm. The cause for my excitement was that, as a recruit, I had the luxury of attending the intimate and candid halftime meeting of the great Alabama team.

Halftime is a pivotal event for a football team – when problems get worked out, strategies and counter-attacks are formed, and, sometimes, a little (or a lot) of anger and excitement get in the way. So for a young lad to have the chance to see the great Bear Bryant give his team hell at halftime for a bad showing was truly a once-in-a-lifetime event. I learned a lesson that day that I have tried to embrace for the past 39 years.

The players and assistant coaches reached the locker room long before Coach Bryant, and all hell broke loose. Coaches were screaming, players were pointing fingers and pushing each other. There was general mayhem and turmoil. In a split second all that changed. Coach Bryant, with his slower than molasses swagger and speech, finally entered the room some 5-7 minutes after all the commotion had started. The place went deadly, eerily, silent in a flash. The great man had entered the room.

You know the saying that describes someone with great charisma? "When they walk into the room you know they are there." Well that was certainly true of Coach Bryant. The locker room went still in a way that made the group that was raising Cain a few minutes earlier look silly somehow.

Then the most amazing thing of all happened. Coach Bryant began to address the team about the first-half performance, and he could barely be heard. His speech was measured, sure, and at a volume that required effort to be heard. I was a little disappointed at first until I became spellbound by the natural greatness of the man. I could sense that he was getting the attention of his team by making them **strain** to hear him. He was making it **their job to hear him**.

Even back then, what was clear to me about this born-leader was that his way was different from everything around him. *Above the fray*. Out of the box.

Coach Bryant did not get into a yelling and screaming contest like his assistant coaches had. As a matter of fact, he did **just the opposite**. Not only did he speak in a low, muted tone, but his message was just as remarkable. He told his team they were too good to play like they had in the first half. He told his team they were too classy to play like they had in the first half. He told his team they were the royalty of college football. He then ordered the players to report to their position coaches and get ready for the second half.

At the end of the halftime, the Alabama players were ten feet tall. They slaughtered South Carolina in the second half.

The point is this: You have to know how to deliver a message. You have to know how to deliver a message to your most important customer, your teammates, in the way that is the most effective given your style. Yelling and screaming and kicking and threatening are never going to work, even if the subject requires an intense approach. Negative reinforcement, like the kind employed by the Alabama assistant coaches in the locker room before Coach Bryant arrived, might work periodically in sports from time to time, but it is **never** going to be effective in business long-term.

> **Communicate with dignity and respect.**
>
> **If you yell at someone they will only hear the sound – NOT the words.**

PART FOUR:

WINNING THE EXTERNAL CUSTOMER

If you do Part Two correctly and learn to
manage yourself –

If you do Part Three correctly and effectively
build a team –

THE EXTERNAL CUSTOMER WILL KNOCK
THE DOOR DOWN TO DO BUSINESS
WITH YOU!

THE PSYCHOLOGY OF CUSTOMER SERVICE

In order to build a strong sales staff you and your people must buy into the psychology of customer service. Webster's Dictionary defines **psychology** as **"the science of emotions, behavior, and the mind."** Therefore it follows that your company should have as a principal goal:

We will embrace customer service with our emotions, our behavior, and our minds.

In Regard to Emotions:
You and your staff cannot **display** overly sensitive reactions to people and events. No one can change the fact that disgruntled people, difficult people and un-reasonable people are going to come along every once

in awhile. We cannot change the fact that unexpected things are going to happen which make simple things complicated. What we CAN CHANGE and CONTROL is our emotional response to these situations.

DIFFICULT AND STRESSFUL THINGS ARE ALWAYS GOING TO HAPPEN – SO WHY GO TO PIECES WHEN THEY DO??

Make this statement to yourself:

I will be confronted with issues and people that are difficult and outside the norm. *Just accepting that such things are going to happen is half the battle.*

Next, make this statement to yourself:

I will control my emotions and solve whatever dilemma comes along – with battlefield nerves. *I WILL NOT fall into the currently fashionable and pathetic thinking that says that every uncomfortable situation makes you the victim. I am in charge.*

In Regard to Behavior:
You and your staff must accept and embrace the fact that behavior is contagious. If the general behavior in your firm is bad, then bad behavior is going to spread and will unfortunately continue to be bad because that has become the norm.

For example, if someone in your company frequently behaves like an idiot when a customer service issue comes up – and gets away with it – then others will do the same.

If someone behaves with calm and cool and poise like my former operations manager, Jeanie Gammon, it will have a positive effect on everybody.

In Regard To The Mind:
You have got to have customer service **at the forefront of everyone's mind.**

You and your people must always think about things from the customer's standpoint.

- Does our business setting look professional and organized?
- Are the customers names spelled correctly on our greeting board?
- Did we change the company voice recording for the upcoming holiday?

These operational details can become embarrassing situations if your people do not keep the customer in mind.

In addition, your staff must be willing to **keep their minds open** to suggestions for improvement. They must be ready to receive continuous feedback from you, each other, and the customers about their performance without taking it personally or in a resentful manner.

As we have explored earlier, overcoming the prevalent "thin-skinned attitude" is tough to accomplish in today's business world. It is amazing how we all tend to run from help regarding our business performance and behavior. We willingly read every kind of self-help book and join self-improvement groups on every kind of issue, yet we turn ourselves into china when a manager wants to address us on some improvement we could make in the workplace.

In today's environment, if someone wants to suggest to a colleague how to get better at golf or to share a new way to lose weight or a sure-fire way to get a date or how to learn speed-reading or how to quit smoking or how to get prettier toenails, most people will listen. But something happens to these open help-seekers when they get to work.

Remember, your delivery of business-related, self-improvement messages must be skillful and tactful. It takes the proper formula to deliver a message to a fellow associate in the form of constructive criticism. Your company needs a protocol for how and when to deliver critiques of behavior or performance.

AmSouth Mortgage was the greatest in the world at getting people to embrace the psychology of customer service. In no small part this was due to the company-wide customer service workshops in which all employees across the South participated. After these events, you saw changes in people that were palpable. This company's commitment to improvement manifested itself at every branch and level.

In the Louisville, Kentucky office we had an extraordinary synergy. We discussed every matter that did not go smoothly in the following fashion: *"I had a terrible time on the Jones file – Mr. Smith was the realtor and he badgered the heck out of me. He acted ugly and destroyed me on my customer evaluation, which is going to kill my bonus, even though I tried like the devil on the file and closed it in two weeks."*

Following this, one of our teammates would respond; *"Smith is a very nervous individual. The key to him is this – you have got to stay AHEAD of him on the phone calls! The next time you have a deal with him see to it that he never calls you first. If you stay ahead of him and inform him—OVER inform him—he will be a teddy bear."*

The first associate would take the advice matter-of-factly and accept it, and we would go on to the next issue with no emotional uproar—WHAT A GREAT GROUP!

On the other hand, I have been in settings where this exchange could cause a fistfight. The difference: One group did not have customer service on their minds, or in their behavior or emotions. The other did. The customer was more important than insignificant personal feelings.

The Psychology of Customer Service:

We will embrace customer service with our emotions, our behavior, and our minds.

WAIT HERE FOR THE NEXT AVAILABLE TELLER

How many times have you seen this sign in a bank? You have probably experienced this many times. You are waiting to make a deposit, or other transaction with the bank, you are standing in line, and you are in a hurry.

You are in a hurry because you have things to do. You have to drop off, pick up, go by, get, take and do all sorts of stuff on your busy day – a day that can go good or bad if anything takes more time than you planned. If you get stuck dropping off some papers, or going to visit a client, or picking up some prescription medicine, you are behind for the rest of the day. Each event hinges upon timeliness. If you get behind anywhere, you are going to be behind everywhere – at each subsequent appointment.

143

Because of your busy schedule you are nervous and annoyed by the "wait here for the next available teller" instructions. You are nervous and annoyed because the "next available teller" is coming out of a potential population of ONE. There is only ONE teller on the job at present and you have five people ahead of you, one of whom is having 1,412 quarters put into $10 paper sleeves. The "one available teller" who is also the "next available teller" is working her fanny off to take care of everybody!

Anxiously, you look around the bank and you notice that there are 4-9 idle bank representatives in the assistant manager area. They are not part of the "next available teller" pool. They are, however, NOT busy. That is why, of course, they will NOT make eye contact with you. They do NOT want you to know that they know, that you know, that they could wait on you if they really wanted to. So they act like they are busy or like they don't see you.

Here is another example of the **disconnect** that we talked about in **Beware of Smiling Faces** – alive and well in its purest form. Without doubt, this bank with the overextended "next available teller" also has a grand and enticing advertising campaign, one that awes us with the incredible customer service that the bank provides. But in reality, it is just another bank, another company that says one thing and does another.

In the end this bank slogan is just another rendition of all the meaningless adages in the customer service world of today. It is the same old story over and over and over again. They all *"talk the* (customer service) talk" but they sure don't *"walk the walk."*

The real tragedy of this story is that the bank misses an opportunity here to proudly provide what the customer **really** wants—SERVICE! The opportunity is standing right in front of the manager's faces and they can't even see it. They can't see it because most of the industry handles things THE SAME WAY.

Just imagine if the assistant managers took this opportunity, ran over willingly, and gladly served the customers who were waiting.

Just imagine the attitude and appreciation of the customers in the long teller line, if the efficiency of this bank made their long day go smoother.

What if the assistant managers assisted the young, rattled, teller to get her work done, to ensure that she didn't show a huffy attitude to the customers? She might become less rattled, even enthusiastic!

With help, the young, less-rattled, teller would have a better day and project a more pleasant attitude to the customers. With some assistance, the young and enthusiastic teller would develop a better vibe about the company and her fellow workers.

Additionally, the manager who has stepped up to serve the waiting customers, has gained a better sense of how to more effectively staff the teller line.

What if you ran a bank where no one had to wait in line like cattle? What if you managed a bank where the people were greeted and helped by ALL the bank personnel and there were no **rules** against helping the external customer or a fellow worker?

**Look at your business
through the
CUSTOMERS' EYES**

NEGATIVE CUSTOMER SERVICE RESPONSES

To provide excellent customer service, you MUST gain a valid and candid picture of how you perform in **the customer's eye**. At the end of the day, the customer's appraisal of your performance is far more important than your own. A successful leader constantly seeks candid and honest insights into the REAL opinions of the company's external customers. Seeing a customer's experience through the customer's eyes is like having the combination to the safe at Fort Knox—IF you know how to use it correctly.

Most companies delivering a product, whose implementation depends on good customer service, have some sort of **customer service evaluation form**. These forms encourage customers to rate the performance of

147

the company personnel. Researching the usage and impact of such forms, a Harvard School of Business study shows the following:

• For every ten successful transactions that result in a **positive customer service response**, the effect will be as follows: Two to four of the ten customers who gave you a positive response will tell one to three other people about the good service they experienced with your company.

This means that for every ten completely smooth transactions, you have generated a **maximum radiation of 12 instances of good will**. (Four of your customers have told three people each— this is the **maximum radiation effect**).

• For each **unpleasant or unfavorable customer response**, the principal involved will tell 10-12 people about his or her bad experience, and those 10-12 will each tell 1-3 of their buddies or associates.

This means you have generated as many as **36 potential customers from one transaction who now think you are an idiot**. Bad news is always more interesting – and travels faster – than good news.

Do the math! If you generate good will to a maximum of 12 outsiders from 10 positive service responses, but you generate bad press to 36 outsiders from 1 negative response that means **it takes 30 positive responses to make up for the one negative response**. And that is just to break even!

Now the good news! The disgruntled customer, the guy who generates 36 bad references, is really the **golden egg**. Think about it. If you can satisfy a disgruntled customer, handle his concerns, and win him over in a positive manner, he will tell 10-12 people about your responsiveness—and the satisfactory way you resolved his problems. Those 10-12 people will each tell 1-3 people about your special treatment of their buddy, spreading more good will for your company. **More importantly, you have eliminated the potential 36 people who would otherwise hear the bad news**, conclude that you are incompetent, and vow never to do business with you!

You must personally follow up on all negative customer service evaluations. This one action can greatly impact the reputation of your company. Be certain that your people understand this. Do not let your teammates dismiss a bad customer service review with the explanation so popular today: *"That guy* (the customer) *was a jerk."*

IT DOES NOT MATTER IF THE GUY WAS A JERK. What does matter is that you follow up, win that disgruntled customer over, and keep him from infecting all those he knows with a bad commentary on your company! Again, see to it that your people understand this. Some never get it.

You or your manager should personally call each customer who does not give you glowing reviews. People are truly surprised and delighted when you take the time to call them, take their feedback seriously, and **let them know how important they are to you**. There is nothing more effective you can do as a salesperson than making a customer feel important.

Take time to explain to all of your staff the importance of follow-up on customer complaints. Make sure your teammates understand the method to this madness – the way that it makes fans out of potential naysayers and builds a large reservoir of good will.

Some staff members may initially dismiss the customer service response dynamic as just another forum for criticizing them. Help them to see this as the golden opportunity that it is – **a path they can follow to achieve excellence in their job functions**. For example, if they are constantly receiving poor ratings on their phone response times, they need only accept the reality of this and work to correct it. As soon as they make a few improvements and experience **the sweet taste of great customer evaluation responses**, their anxieties about criticism will disappear.

> **Pay attention to comments on customer response forms.**
>
> **Seek to satisfy the disgruntled customer.**
>
> **Want to be great at your job? The customer will show you how.**

SIGNS, SIGNS, SIGNS: HOW NOT TO INSULT THE CUSTOMER

My gorgeous wife and I recently visited a doctor's office. We noticed that for some reason the wonderful medical practitioners of today feel it is necessary to insult their existing and prospective customers. The signs that they display in their patient waiting areas make this disdain very evident. On our recent visit we observed, or rather, were assaulted by the following signs:

- $25 charge for returned checks.
- Cancellations must be made 24 hours in advance. Failure will result in a $30 cancellation fee.
- Co-pays are Due IMMEDIATELY.
- Cellular telephones MAY NOT be used in our waiting area.

- Please do NOT remove magazines from the lounge area.

All this in the same office! Wouldn't it be enlightening to explain to the office manager what those messages might mean to the customers? Wouldn't it be an eye-opener to tell the doctor how some people might interpret these signs?

If I had such an opportunity, I would translate the meaning of these signs in the following manner:

• **Returned Check Charge. Translation:** You are either too stupid to balance a checkbook or enough of a con artist to try to hang some bad paper on poor ole' Doc.

• **Cancellation Charge. Translation:** Our time is more valuable than yours. It is okay for you to sit in the lobby and wait for three hours, but it is not okay for you not to sit in the lobby and wait. YOU MUST WAIT!

• **Immediate Co-Pay. Translation:** Unlike any other business in America you must pay us for our services and then wait to get them. Since you can't balance a checkbook; you do try to hang bad paper; and you don't let us know when you cancel appointments; pay us NOW because we don't trust you.

• **No Cell Phones. Translation:** You are not important enough to try to conduct business or take care of family matters while you are in our office. There is nothing that a dummy like you can do on the phone that is more important than completing your required three hours wait in our lobby.

• **Don't Remove Magazines. Translation:** You filthy, check-bouncing, cell-phone-talking, no-insurance-having slut. Times are tough. If you steal this $1.95 edition of *Diabetes Today*, the doctor will fall on hard times.

Think about the messages you are sending your customers. Look around at the trappings of your work setting. What do they communicate to your customers? Do you project the image of a company that is sensitive and respectful, or does it appear to be arrogant and condescending?

> **Think about the way you present yourself –
> your team – your company –
> to the external customer.**

Not to pick on the health services profession, but look at the way they handle the parking spots at hospitals. The doctors and clergy get to park right up front, next to the hospital! The sick people have to park back in the back and crawl to the front door!

**Don't insult
decent people
who want to do
business with you.**

**A sign on the outside
gives a hint of
what's really inside.**

153

DON'T WASH YOUR DIRTY LAUNDRY IN PUBLIC

Over the years, I have been amazed at the pathetic way people in the mortgage industry sometimes convey information to the external customer. It often consists of a litany of excuses and cry-babying.

Unfortunately, for the people who deliver these worn-out phrases the result in the eyes of the customer is this: **You are just making yourself look weak.**

I am sure you are aware of, and have probably been subjected to, some of the tired old excuses used in the mortgage lending business.

> "I am so sorry this is taking so long, but the underwriter is nit-picking your loan."

"The closing attorney should have supplied you with that information."

"The loan has been held up because the appraiser is too busy to get to the house and appraise it."

The above phrases have similar versions in most other industries. Some of these include:

"I'm sorry this is taking so long but our chef is new."

"We can't verify your present automobile loan payoff or balance without a written request."

"I am sorry but the clerk neglected to include the undercoating for your new car in the final price."

Notice that with all these excuses, it is someone else's fault!

Not only do I find these messages offensive from the receiver's standpoint, but I also find them offensive from the standpoint of the deliverer. What I mean is that I would never lay the blame off on someone else who is a member of my organization. What good does that possibly do? Does it make you look better? Rarely – if at all. But it also makes your team look worse.

Here's a football analogy. You're interviewed on camera after a game and you explain your team's loss by saying, "I am a great running back, but our linemen can't block worth a damn." Do you think the linemen are now going to be motivated to start blocking harder?

This is a critical point in learning how to carry your-self in the proper manner within a sales organization. It is an important and fundamental step in building a dynamic customer service team. **Defend your team** and show your customer that you have the **strength and influence** within your organization to get the job done in spite of all the little, and sometimes not so little, nuisances that come along in every business.

When a successful firm runs into one of the bottlenecks mentioned on the previous page, **the customer NEVER hears about it!**

There may be some blood spilling inside the office but to the customer it is all seamless. When you handle problems in this way you are giving the customer what they want! What they don't want is to waste time hearing about all the problems that are taking place.

My wife and I recently celebrated our twentieth anniversary. We were ready to do the town and one restaurant in our city proclaims that they are the place for "special occasions." Since a twentieth anniversary is a pretty "special occasion" we chose that particular location. We were warmly greeted, seated at a great table, and waited twenty-five minutes before our waiter showed up. I was already furious but the situation was exacerbated with the tardy waiter's greeting..."*I have a table for 16 on the other side of the room so I am awfully busy.*" I didn't give a damn about his other table – I was at my twentieth anniversary dinner with the woman of my dreams! I wanted to kill the guy.

Things got worse in the next 40 minutes, and we ended up walking out. The point is this: if you are about special occasions, and someone makes a reservation for a 20th anniversary dinner, you should:

1. Know about it
2. Know that your company is about "special occasions"
3. Understand that the other logistic problems are not the concern of your "special occasion" customer.

Excuse making is generally done to take the monkey off the back of the messenger and lay the blame on someone else. In the midst of a delay or snafu, it's used as a way to pass off fault and make oneself look as good as possible.

What **excuse making really does is make the messenger look as bad as possible**. The real signal you send to the customer when you employ this strategy is that **you are too weak to handle the situation**. You are not in control of your business environment.

How many times have I heard the lament, *"I don't know why so and so doesn't do business with us anymore, the big screw up on the last deal wasn't my fault!"* Some people just don't get it. **It doesn't matter to Mr. So-and-So whose fault it was – he just knows not to use your firm anymore.**

Work these things out, **especial**ly the ones you know you can resolve, behind the scenes without getting the external customer involved or informed. If there is "dirty laundry" to be washed, do it out of the sight and hearing of the customer. If you do this effectively, your customers will have the impression that your operation is smoother than the competition, even though you have the same challenges as everyone else in your line of business.

Why tell the customer how lousy and incompetent your company is? Give your customer the correct impression that you can handle the bumpy roads better than others. Better yet, don't even take them down the bumpy roads.

> **Don't share
> internal delays and mistakes
> with the external customer.**
>
> **Handle problems internally.
> Keep the
> customer's ride
> smooth.**

THE JOE BTFSPLK CUSTOMER

We have all had problem customers. In fact, there is one kind of customer for whom you have to set up an ICCU. This means an Intensive Customer Care Unit.

The ICCU is for the problem, disgruntled, unlucky customer for whom nothing goes right. This is the guy who behaves terribly about everything; who argues every issue; and for whom everything truly does go wrong! All of this is intensified because he has **the worst luck in the world**.

I've named this guy after the character in the classic Li'l Abner comic strips, **Joe Btfsplk**, a poor soul who walked around, literally, with a dark cloud over his head. Everything always went wrong for him – **AND for** anybody near him!

Unfortunately, this type of customer can create the same dark cloud over you. If you don't handle Joe Btfsplk properly he will do a lot of harm to the image of your business when he is turned loose on the public.

When you or someone on your team has identified a Joe Btfsplk customer, make everyone aware of his existence. Be especially sensitive to everything that comes up while you are dealing with him. You have got to get this guy on the other side of the close without any major damage. Joe Btfsplk is a weapon of mass destruction for any customer service business.

To give you an example of a Joe Btfsplk customer, let me relate it from my own experience in the mortgage industry.

Some borrowers that come through just seem to be star-crossed like Joe. For who knows what reason, even in a highly efficient operation, everything goes wrong with this guy's account. To begin with, our appraiser somehow gets the wrong phone number for setting up Joe's home appraisal. So the appraisal gets held up for two weeks until somebody figures out what went wrong.

Next, the closing is mistakenly assigned to the wrong closing attorney and, inexplicably, the closer transposes twenty-five to fifty-two, so the loan amount shows up as $352,000 when it should have been $325,000.

To further confuse the situation, the loan was supposed to be a 30-year fixed but somewhere along the way, Joe mentioned a 15-year loan, and his loan was incorrectly processed that way.

After all this trouble, you have the extra complication of Joe. First, he brings the wrong papers to the closing. Next, when he is told to present his home insurance policy, he pulls out the auto policy for his car. Everything is a mess.

And you can bet that **AFTER** the loan FINALLY closes things are going to continue to go haywire. In Joe's case, his escrow account gets messed up, and the lender sends his tax payments to the wrong municipality. In another of our "Joe" loans, the tax payment was sent to Jefferson County, Alabama, instead of Jefferson County, Kentucky!

Everybody in the customer service business has had an experience with trying to close a deal with a Joe. There are two certainties about a Joe Btfsplk customer:

1. There will be others. Just because you and your staff get through this the first time, don't think you are done with this kind of "Joe" experience.

2. You cannot let Joe go back out into the world unless – every step of the way – you do everything in your power to make him happy.

Whenever it becomes clear that a Joe customer is in the house, initiate your plan of defense. React as soon as possible—make sure everybody knows about Joe and has manned their battle stations. This is the time for consistent and enthusiastic teamwork. This is NOT the time for the "that's not my table" mode of behavior. Everybody needs to stay alert, think, and check TWICE about every issue that comes up with Joe.

Joe and all future Joes must be put in the ICCU
– Intensive Customer Care Unit –
to prevent painful and embarrassing situations.

Remember the formula: the bad customer service evaluation generates 36 people who know that you handled one customer poorly. Well, Joe will send these figures through the roof!! One hundred or more people will know about Joe's experience, because people who know Joe, love to hear his stories.

**Be on the lookout
for Joe Btfsplk.**

Always put Joe in the ICCU.

**BE READY
for the next Joe**

The Intensive Customer Care Unit – ICCU –
EVERYBODY watches Joe Btfsplk.

THE STORY OF RUTH
— FIXING IT
FOR EVERYBODY

The key element, the crucial element, in building my mortgage business was the people we were fortunate enough to have on our team. One of those people was Ruth Wathen, a truly unique and singular character when it came to providing customer service.

Customer service is not what Ruth did—it was who she **was**. This is a story about Ruth and her unequaled approach to getting things done for people.

Roger Connors, Tom Smith and Craig Hickman co-authored a tremendous book about customer service titled *The Oz Principle*. The book tells stories of support personnel who go above and beyond the usual to get things done in tough situations. For example, there is the story of a truck driver who finds himself in a real dilemma. His company has developed a cutting edge product and sold the initial run to a very important customer. The truck driver MUST get the goods delivered by a Sunday. However, his truck breaks down on Saturday, and he is still one day in travel-time away from the customer.

To make a very long story short, the driver takes it upon himself to use his personal negotiation skills to rent another truck in the area; he has his truck unloaded and the new truck loaded; and, he delivers the goods on time. This driver's superior service leads to a huge contract between his employer and the very satisfied customer.

Connors, Smith and Hickman call this type of behavior "fixing it" in their "steps to accountability" formula for success. This story illustrates what people can do if they are empowered and encouraged to use their God-given skills, and are not dumbed-down with over-management.

Ruth Wathen performed similar acts of exemplary customer service – too many to mention. One story stood out as an example of her "fixing it" – actually took "fixing it" to a whole new level. Ruth's actions in a difficult situation warranted accolades and praise beyond the normal. This motivated me to do the appropriate thing. I wrote to Connors, Hickman and Smith and related how Ruth's actions reflected *The Oz Principle*. I proposed that she had actually **added** a new level of accountability to the concept. The following is my letter to these authors about Ruth:

Sirs:

Your book is marvelous. My industry, residential mortgage originations, is the birthplace of the PVS (poor, victimized salesperson) syndrome. However, one of our teammates has risen above to such an extent that I believe she has invented a whole new category in the steps to accountability.

Ours is a new firm formed from industry experience as well as a determination to do it right and be "above the fray" in terms of telling our external customers the truth. With marketing efforts like our logo which states "No voice mail during office hours" we are making great strides in market share acquisition in a down market. Mostly because our people don't believe it is a down market.

Recently, we had the good fortune to originate a mortgage for the area's finest custom home-builder. His wife just happens to be one of our area's top three producing real estate agents. These are dream customers for any mortgage company because of the referral potential, and we got the business on the new purchase of their personal home.

They purchased an exclusive unit in a fabulous new high-rise condo. We had the loan approved so quickly that the builder and his realtor wife asked, "Can you do loans this quickly for our customers as well?" In my stupidity I answered "Of course, it's my company, we are in complete control of the process—we don't have under-

writers in West Iowa or voice mail or any of the nonsense you have to go through with other lenders! Just call us and we'll take care of it!"

I came back to the office with all my tales of triumph in the battlefield. Ruth took the loan package and prepared it for closing a short one week later. I left the office on Wednesday, July 19th to start a short vacation, and that's when the trouble started.

When a residential mortgage is approved, lenders require a flood certification that determines if the property is in a flood plain and therefore requires flood insurance to be carried by the borrower. When my customer found out that our flood cert showed this property required flood insurance he went ballistic. He told the staff "I thought you told me you were in control of your company, why in world do I need flood insurance?? The other lenders in the project don't require it!" All the while this is happening I am off on vacation.

The other lenders that had closed previous transactions in the project had secured an engineering waiver on the flood certification since it was a high-rise condo. We could not do that because the dummy (me) had already pre-sold the loan to a lender that required flood certifications from a particular agency and would accept no others. Even though I was out of town, I just knew Ruth would find a solution. I thought of the truck-driver who overcame every obstacle to make an initial delivery of a new product and just knew Ruth had the same stuff. However, if this did not get worked out, it would be a business disaster given the resultant flak and ammunition for my competitors.

Ruth got in touch with the general engineer in charge of the entire development and found out that a flood cert **clearing** the property of the need for flood insurance existed. The cert and clearing had been done by FEMA (Federal Emergency Management Agency) **BUT WAS NEVER RECORDED.**

Ruth obtained a copy of the report and waiver, GOT IT RECORDED, and had FEMA send a letter to ALL flood reporting agencies so that NO OTHER LENDER WOULD HAVE THIS PROBLEM ON THIS PROJECT AGAIN.

A new form of accountability—FIX IT FOR EVERYBODY!!!

What did this do for us other than getting the loan closed smoothly? Should we have kept this information in a lock box and let others go through the same agony when the problem came up again? We sure could have.

We thought not and here is why:

• Why act small? Why not do something good for the community and separate ourselves from the competition?

- *Why not set a higher form of example for our industry? An industry which suffers from practices of late such as predatory lending and seedy, misleading customer service and advertising.*

- *Why not do something nice for someone? One of our existing or previous clients might move into the building. We would be doing them, because of Ruth, an anonymous good deed.*

- *Ruth created goodwill with the engineer and the project manager. Who knows what that can lead to on future projects they might put together?*

- *Most importantly, Ruth did what her heart told her to do:* **Fix it for your fellow man***.*

Sincerely,
Paul Karem

It never hurts to carry yourself with class and do the right thing. I can assure you a lot of people in this industry would not have handled things like Ruth Wathen. However, that's because Ruth is innovative and exemplary – and she knew she was empowered to act decisively to solve problems for our company. Her quick action resulted in millions of dollars of referrals from the cast of characters involved. All because a great person took the "high road" and did not act in a compromising or small-minded way.

Choose the "Ruth" way
of doing things:

Fix it for EVERYBODY!

Above the Fray

NERVE-WRACKING ISSUES

Everyone recognizes the pressures and tensions inherent in business today. Somehow computers and cell phones and pagers and car phones and fax machines and emails have failed to make our jobs and lives easier – they have made some things harder.

Sometimes today's pressures and tensions spill over as ugly behavior on the part of the support people who are the day-to-day lifeblood of your business. It is very important to understand the pressures that impact your staff. You have to make sure your people don't lose their edge – their mojo for the work. You must make sure that pressures have not built up over time that might cause one or more of your people to lose their enthusiasm. Enthusiasm makes people with supposedly

NO potential outperform people who have TONS of potential. This fact is significant to you as a manager.

To provide superior customer service, you must be sure your people are aware of the pressures experienced by the **external customer**.

Sometimes, in fact most of the time, the external customers' pressures are more intense than those of the service provider. For example: In the mortgage business, the mortgage processor is the person who does all the number crunching and brainwork. The processor handles most of the annoying details – like getting everyone together to schedule the closing. An excellent processor can carry as many as 30-50 loans in their processing pipeline. That means 30-50 buyers, sellers and realtors are calling everyday to get progress reports on loans. Such a load can become very heavy on a high-volume processor.

But here is the other side of the story: The realtor's job can sometimes make the processor's job look like a walk in the park. It is the realtor who has to drive clients around in a car and show them various homes on the weekend. It is the realtor who has to watch their children if the clients come from out of town and have to go on other appointments. It is the realtor who takes the clients to lunch and listens to their exasperated ramblings about the trials of moving and not quickly finding a new home.

It is the realtor who recommends the mortgage company to a buyer. The mortgage company's performance reflects on the realtor as well. My support people knew this. My support people knew how the customer, in this case – the realtor – made a living.

And my support people knew that we were NOT in the mortgage business – we were in the realtor and borrower service business. **It was our job to know and embrace the customer and the customer's concerns.**

Embracing the customer's concerns...
- The bartender understands that sometimes he has to be a father confessor to a troubled patron.

- The airline ticket agent considers that the anxious and impatient flyer just might be trying to get home to a child or spouse with health problems so she is calm and helpful.

- The banker understands that the elderly lady doesn't hear very well, so it doesn't seem so horrible that he must explain the conditions of her certificate of deposit 14 times.

- The gatekeeper (receptionist) at the doctor's office considers that the pain the person on the other end of the phone is describing might be life threatening and realizes that this is a little more important than her lunch.

In general, the customer's needs usually rank higher in importance than the service provider's issues. If your people embrace this philosophy, your company will be **great.**

UNDERSTAND the customer
and you will

UNDERSTAND the problem
and YOUR problem

will GO AWAY

THE
OTHER CUSTOMER

When you are great at your job more people know about it than you think. Think about **"The Story of Ruth"** and consider how much unsolicited business we got from Ruth doing such a fantastic job on a relatively small deal. You never know who else is involved and how many people are affected.

We have all heard the stories. For example: A gentleman in Louisville, a developer, was involved in a lawsuit as the plaintiff. He failed in his action and the court's ruling was against him. However, in the process he noticed, and was impressed by, the performance of his adversary's attorney. Now that attorney represents the builder's sizeable company.

Certainly you can make the statement that the opposing attorney never considered this lawsuit as a forum for winning new customers. Because of his dash, skill, and effective manner, winning the new customer is exactly what he accomplished.

You never know whose eyes are watching you. In the mortgage industry, as I have previously explained, the key referral source is the realtor. The realtor who represents the buyer of a home is the one that plays a key role in helping their buyer select a mortgage lender. But, there is also a realtor in the transaction who represents the seller of the home. The realtor on that side of the transaction is called the listing realtor.

The listing realtor is responsible for bringing the transaction to fruition while handling all the issues relevant to the seller, like sale price, closing date, when the buyer takes possession of the home and similar issues.

When my company handled financing, we afforded the listing realtor every courtesy that we provided to the selling realtor. We presented progress reports and updates on the processing of the file to both sets of realtors, even though the selling realtor was the one who brought us the case. Many times on customer service reviews, we have secured glowing commentary from the selling realtor. Just as many times, we have received laudatory comments like the following from a listing realtor: *"I have never been so well informed before by the mortgage company when I was representing the seller—I never had that experience with another mortgage company."*

180

In my business, we realized, early on, that eventually a listing realtor will be acting as a selling realtor – representing a buyer who needs a mortgage. Every time we saw a listing agent on a contract presented by our borrower we viewed that as a new customer possibility. The greatest thing about this is – we did not have to go out and find that new customer! **The existing realtor/ customer who brought the deal to us in the first place brought the other realtor along as well.**

In ways you cannot imagine, every individual with whom your company deals is a referral source. They are part of a family and community. When you perform well on a key transaction, everyone in that person's family will know about it. When you treat family members with respect and dignity and courtesy and professionalism, you have won the strongest trust there is. The trust that comes from treating a family member with honor and integrity is the strongest loyalty you can build. Keep in mind that everybody you deal with has a family or, at least, a circle of influence.

Trust, truth and dignity are the strongest magnets for attracting new business from sources of which you are not even aware. I have heard the following kinds of comments many times in my career: "I am bringing my financing to you because of the advice you gave my brother." "I heard about you from my cousin, she said you were a class act!" "My dad's partner said I should be sure and come to you. He said you would treat me right."

Frequently, these comments referred to something we advised a customer not to do. By that I mean we might have advised someone against refinancing their home because it made better sense to do things another way. We cost ourselves **that deal**, but we won the customer's sphere of influence. This is called telling the customer **the truth**. You can't get caught up in the chase of the deal – winning the customer's trust is more important.

**Tell the customer
the truth.
You might lose
THAT deal,
but
you win the
CUSTOMER'S TRUST**

**AND – the OTHER
customer.**

Don't Assume The Buyer Knows Anything

Have you ever felt dismissed by a customer service provider? I am talking about the guy who makes you feel stupid.

• I am talking about the person who goes through something too fast, like the lawyer who puts a bunch of papers in front of you and asks you to sign them all. I am talking about the car rental agent who gives you 15 forms and has you initial and sign 47 different places while she is talking at warp speed.

• I am talking about the person at the hospital who checks you in for an outpatient procedure, when you are already nervous, and she goes through too many forms too fast because she is actually concerned about

183

getting X number of patients checked in before her lunch break.

A great strategy for these types, from the customer's point of view, is simply to tell them what you want. Instruct them on how you want to be treated. If you want everything explained just say so. "Wait a minute...don't go so fast...I need to understand what is going on" is a great way to get the person you are dealing with redirected.

But we are not talking about how the customer should handle these types. We are looking at this issue from the standpoint of being the service provider. This whole section concerns how to treat the external customer.

Here are some useful strategies for communicating successfully with your customer:

Never, ever, be dismissive of a customer. Sometimes it can appear you are being dismissive when actually you are not. You might be in a hurry to get everything done with a customer because you have assumed that the buyer knows what you are talking about—when in fact the buyer does NOT know what you are talking about. You come off as arrogant and dismissive. Keep this fact in mind: just because you have explained something a million times does not mean that the next person you are explaining the same thing to has any idea what you are talking about.

In the mortgage business, we are required by law to give our customers a full estimate of all the costs involved in a mortgage. Included in those costs are amounts for taxes and insurance, which have nothing to do with the lender or the mortgage. A home is going to be taxed, and the homeowner will be wise to have insurance, regardless of whether or not there is a mortgage on the house.

Once, a friend of a friend came in to see me about getting a mortgage. I gave him my best quote and the aforementioned estimate with all the costs. Two days later, I found out that he had selected another lender. When I lose a deal, I am driven to find out the reason. I called the gentleman and asked him why he had selected another lender. His response was a great lesson on **understanding** the customer. He said, *"We really wanted to go with your firm but your costs on insurance were too high."* I almost fell off the chair. However, I told him I understood and learned my lesson.

The lesson is this: I did not fully anticipate my customer's need for information and clarification. The insurance costs were **NOT** part of **my firm's** fees. They were simply part of the total cost of the transaction for the borrower, I had to put some kind of figure on the form to represent the insurance cost, even though it was not part of the lender's fee structure. I chose a moderate fee like you would see from State Farm or Allstate. The other lender showed a minimal, almost unobtainable forecast of the insurance fee, so the borrower selected the other lender since everything else was the same.

I had assumed the borrower knew that the fees for insurance were simply an estimate, and that he would personally have to select the insurance carrier. Mistakenly, I assumed that he knew that the cost of insurance was, in the end, up to him. All this happened, and I lost the deal, because I did not take time with the customer to **explain** the taxes and insurance **more clearly**. All this happened and I lost the deal, because I had been over this form a million times, and assumed the borrower knew as much about it as I did. NEVER again did I lose a loan for that reason.

**Take time
with your customers.**

**Be happy to explain
and clarify.**

**Don't assume
they know as much
as you know.**

RECEPTIONIST

You are not going to have an outstanding customer service organization without an outstanding receptionist. No way.

The impression, the first impression, made by the receptionist to your external customers, cannot be overstated. A *smile in the voice*, a cordial and helpful attitude, and a familiarity with customers has a value that cannot be quantified. This contrasts with the mumbled, barely understandable greetings that we encounter today.

In the recent past, the receptionist was one of the most carefully filled positions in any industry. What makes it crucial for you today is the fact that your competition no longer recognizes the receptionist's importance. As

187

a matter of fact, most companies do not even have a receptionist. I cannot figure out the logic of that, but it definitely provides YOU with a customer service opportunity.

To experience this lack of a receptionist first hand, call a large mortgage company over the phone for a very enlightening experience. The typical greeting is a festival of prompts – "press one for payoffs" – "press two for your present balance" – "press three for blah, blah, blah." These are the same companies that go on and on in radio and television ads about how great their customer service is, and how important you are to them as a customer.

If they really had a concern about customer service, wouldn't it be easier to hire one, or even two, nice people to answer the phone? Wouldn't it make sense to find one or two people with the qualities of customer warmth and courtesy to greet customers and direct their calls?

The only reasonable explanation for why this is not done more often is that companies have lost touch with the concerns and sensitivities of the customer.

A lot of this applies to your business and those you deal with everyday. You know that because you have tried to call them to get service. The worst I have experienced is our local cable TV company. When the cable goes out, you have to call the customer service department to report the situation.

If I live to be 747 years old, I will never understand

why the cable company calls this department the customer service department. How can it be the "customer service department" when no one will answer the phone? Not only that, you have to listen to a voice-over advertisement starring the CEO of the cable company telling you, for as much as one hour before someone answers the phone, how wonderful their customer service is!

But here is the real kicker. When someone in their horrendously understaffed phone pool finally answers the phone – they are more aggravated than you are! This is because they are exhausted and washed out from dealing all day with all the exhausted and washed out people who have been holding for one hour listening to ads about how great the cable company customer service is! By the time the customers connect with the customer service representative, he or she has simply become the most available target for their frustrations. This is a counterproductive dynamic that is easily remedied.

All you have to do is give the customer some consideration and respect. Make a few calls to your competition and see what you hear. Make a few calls to your own company and see what happens – if you can do it without giving away your cover. Are you greeted warmly? Do you get lost punching buttons in a phone-tree? Are you just hurried into voice mail? If you need some basic information is there a receptionist able to give it to you, or, more importantly, does she seem to care, and is she trying to help? Worst of all, do you get the feeling you are dealing with the gatekeeper? You know the gatekeeper. She's the one who won't let you talk to the doctor.

Open the gate.

Hire
a great
receptionist!

VENDORS

Outside vendors are an important and critical aspect of the success of any business. Regardless of the nature of your business, the attorneys, insurance reps, suppliers, designers, agents, and all vendors specific to your business are, in most cases, just as crucial to the reputation of your business as the internal employee.

We have already explored the ways in which the internal employee or member of your team directly influences the image the public has of your company. Additionally, your vendors often contribute to the impression customers have about your business. This can be both good and bad.

Your vendors effectively expand your horizon and areas of influence. In practice, they are outside agents, who, though not on your payroll, can contribute to the good impression of your company. So that is certainly good.

But, what if one of your vendors makes a damaging impression on your external customer? That is certainly bad. Imagine the Coke rep stocking shelves in the grocery store. He's acting surly and snotty to the shoppers. To these customers he is indistinguishable from the actual employees of the grocery store. To the external customer, they are one and the same.

Perception is reality. If an external customer thinks the workers in a grocery store are snotty and surly, then that customer will choose to go to another store. It doesn't matter to the customer whether the snotty person is an actual employee of the store or a vendor's delivery person who happens to be stocking shelves. Again, to the customer it's all the same.

Make no bones about it – **the external vendor has an important hand in your business**. Let's say the Coke vendor is nice and polite and makes a positive impression on the customers. This Coke vendor generates good will for the store because the customers think, wittingly or unwittingly, that the Coke guy works in the store. If he's nice, it must be a great store!

Your vendors must understand that **you and your customers** – not just you – are customers of the vendor. In the mortgage business, we cannot send an offensive or insulting appraiser to someone's home. We can't use an appraiser who makes comments like *"this place is a dump, there is no way I can appraise it for $400,000!"*

Everyone you deal with has a hand in the impression your company or business makes. To get this under control, accept only the same kind of service-excellence from your vendors that you require from your team. Explain to vendors that they have a hand in your success. If they are not smart enough or sensitive enough to get the gist of this, then get rid of them and find new ones.

To the external customer, your internal employees and external vendors all represent the same company – **the same entity**. When your vendors accept this, you have expanded your arena of influence and added to your company's winning image and good reputation. One of the best things about this approach is that your competitors largely don't get it – it sets you apart from the pack.

**Hold your vendors to the same level
of service excellence that your external customers
demand of you.**

Make them understand that your company sets high customer service goals and is in constant pursuit of exemplary performance.

If you are a successful businessperson you probably have implemented the use of customer service reviews. If you are willing to undergo such constant evaluation, then you need vendors who buy into this approach. Set the standard of excellence that you demand and expect from your vendors. Have your internal team monitor vendor performance just as you ask your external customers to monitor your performance.

Remember: **to the outside customer you and your external vendors are indistinguishable** – ALL reflect on your company. Where possible, include vendors in your service evaluations. Better yet, encourage your vendors to **send YOU** service evaluations so **you** can rate **their** performance.

**Vendors represent
your company.
They can make a good or bad
impression on the external
customer.**

**Enlist your vendors
to contribute to the excellence
of your customer service.**

FINAL SAY
ON THE FRAY

Our deepest fear is NOT that we are inadequate. Our deepest fear is that we are POWERFUL beyond measure.

It is our light, not our darkness that most frightens us. We ask ourselves, who am I to be brilliant, gorgeous, talented and fabulous?

Actually, who are you not to be? You are a child of God. Your playing small doesn't serve the world. There is nothing enlightened about shrinking so that other people won't feel insecure around you.

195

We are born to manifest the glory of God that is within us. It's not just in some of us: It's in EVERYONE.

As we let our own light shine we unconsciously give other people permission to do the same. As we are liberated from our own fear our presence automatically liberates others.

— Marianne Williamson

**You can go one of two ways.
You can be above the fray or
you can be in the fray.**

If you want to be in the fray, there are a lot of people who want you down there with them. Misery loves company. They are all down there waiting for you; the customer hatred reps, the parking-lot vigilantes, Joe Btfsplk. You can be down there with them and even feel self-satisfied about it, or you can be above it all to let your light shine as suggested by Ms. Williamson.

Which way
will you go?

C'mon up!

Above the Fray

SMART STUFF
AND
DUMB STUFF

You never know what you are going to pick up along the way. You never know who or what will supply you with **smart** and helpful ideas, and you never know when you will learn or hear something **dumb**. Here I'll share with you some thoughts on both:

SMART: "You make your own luck."

DUMB: "If you're in business, you better know all about your competitor's business." [This is a waste of time.]

SMART: "Take care of your own business and don't worry about the other guy."

DUMB: "They'll never know the difference." [Overheard at a friend's 50th birthday party – a comment by the bartender regarding changing the requested brand of vodka.]

DUMB: Parking for customers only.

REAL SMART: The book, *Richest Man in Babylon* by George S. Clason.

SMART: "There's ALWAYS a reason." [This is gleaned from the book, *The Five People You Meet in Heaven* by Mitch Albom.] There is ALWAYS a reason when people act troubled or project unhappiness. It helps to know that sometimes it is not you.

SMART: *The God Within Us*; a tape by Wayne Dyer.

DUMB: Any show of temper.

DUMB: Saying the reason that you got a bad customer service review is because "the customer was crazy."

SMART: Thinking you are skillful, resourceful, and talented enough to get a good customer service review from a crazy person.

SMART: Getting the point across without yelling.

SMART: Treating your fellow workers like they are your most important customers.

DUMB: Telling people who work for you that they are not capable of doing something.

DUMB: A message during a 20-30 minute hold with a company recording telling you how important you are as a customer.

DUMB: A restaurant hostess who doesn't smile.

DUMB: Posters of smiling people on the wall in a business where nobody is smiling.

SMART: "The customer is always right—ESPECIALLY when he's wrong."

DUMB: Demanding change of others without cleaning up your own act first.

SMART: Cleaning up your side of the street first.

APPENDIX

Employee Contracts
&
Customer Service Review

Employee Contract 1

Three months have just now passed with Paul Karem Mortgage. Seldom do I take changing jobs lightly. Usually, I agonize over the decision for weeks before I can decide what to do. The description you painted of how a mortgage company should be, as well as reading Above The Fray, made me even more excited to leave the wonderful world of state government and get back to a real life mortgage company.

It's very hard at first to know exactly what an employer wants, other than the basics, of course. But I feel like I'm learning exactly what your looking for in an employee.

I love structure and rules. Without them a company gets out of control. None of us can complete our tasks without the overall help of our coworker. Those who think they do it on their own are crazy! I appreciate Jeanie and Ruth so much for all the help they've given me. They share information and answer questions without hesitation. After working in several different atmospheres (all hostile), I feel the reason your idea of an Underprosinator* has been so successful is due to the ability of sharing and caring among the staff.

Below are a few of the things I want to accomplish or improve upon:

1. Increase my pipeline so there can be a more even distribution of the loans.

2. Take over the investor guides/handbooks to familiarize myself with the huge number of products available.

3. Create a training manual/guide for any future employee of Paul Karem Mortgage. A well trained employee is a happy employee.

4. Produce a good faith estimate that you're going to like.

5. Organize my time better.

6. Keep in mind what your vision of a mortgage company should be.

7. Be able to understand why you do the things you do.

---

*Underprosinator: This is a Paul Karem-ism that means one person handles the file from start to finish.

Employee Contract 2

Paul, you asked me to write a contract about myself, and the analytical person that I am, started to analyze where to begin. I have already set in my mind long before my review came up, what I wanted to accomplish in 1993. I feel that I have done a great job at this point having to learn the Mortgage Business, but now it's time to learn more.

My first goal for 1993 is to have completed an MBA course. I feel I need to further my knowledge of FHA and VA loans. I feel that I have so much to learn in these areas and I want to feel comfortable and more knowledgeable when processing.

I want to keep my processing time within 20 to 30 day approvals, and do my best to fulfill the needs of both customers and agents to build a strong and reliable open line of communication.

The post closing report is one of the tasks that I plan to work very hard to keep them cleared from the report, and just becoming more organized to work harder for the cornerstone award.

Steady planning and hard work is what it will take to accomplish these goals. I take a lot of pride in my work and I am very dedicated to my work. I know I can accomplish these goals by the 1993 year end.

And for my personal life, I plan to have as much fun and enjoy what the New Year may bring for me and my family.

Employee Contract 3

Dear Paul,

When I started with AMSOUTH in May 1991, I wasn't sure of myself as a processor. I have learned and I am still learning so much from this company and from you. I am happy to say "I work for AMSOUTH," and I feel it's the #1 Mortgage Company in Louisville. I feel like I am doing a good job for the company, but I can always do better. My goal this month is to pass the DE test I am taking on Thursday and Friday.

My other goals are as follows:

1. Be a better processor and better support leader for the other processors.

2. Learn to control my temper and not to show my temper to other employees.

3. Take all learning classes available to me.

4. Help with financing seminars given to agents and builders.

I am very dedicated to this company and to you, I just wish that some of the other employees had the same dedication. It's hard to work (when we are busy) and try and stay in a "social attitude." I know that I come in late and I am the fist to admit that I am late. I am really trying to get here on time. But when I do get in I do get to work right away and get my things done and still help others. I can remember working from 8 to 9 at night and the same people working late and others leaving at 5:00 on the dot. Once we do get busy again, I hope that all employees are dedicated and can show that by working late until the work is done. We can't keep this company #1 without the dedication and the teamwork. This is in our mission statement and we need to "practice what we preach." This is a great company and it's the best one that I've had the pleasure of working for.

Employee Contract 4

What I will bring to Paul Karem Mortgage Company

<u>Industry Knowledge</u>
*I bring 25 years of mortgage and banking industry
experience to the position. I have held various positions
including origination, processing and underwriting.
Also, experience in the real estate field as a real estate agent.*

<u>Positive Attitude</u>
*I will bring a positive attitude that can be felt by my
co-workers and by our customers and that will add
to more business and better business relationships.
When writing this contract, I considered making a
list of "job duties." However in a situation such as
this, where the company consists of three people, job
duties may include anything from setting up
computers to taking out the trash. I feel that what
is important is attitude and a willingness to accept that
the job duties will be whatever it takes to make this
business successful. I am committed to making this happen.*

<u>Solid Communication Skills</u>
*I communicate effectively, both verbally and in
writing. This increases efficiency in working with
customers and within our team. I like the idea of
Thursday morning meetings to exchange ideas and
to receive feedback. I value constructive criticism in
an environment where people respect one another
and treat one another in a professional manner.*

Dedication & Loyalty
I am very dedicated and loyal to my employer and co-workers, both within and outside of the office. I am committed to making decisions that add value to the company. When I make a mistake I am willing to admit to that mistake and will do everything necessary to correct it.

Ambition & Self Motivation
I continually look for opportunities to learn and improve my skill sets. I value success.

What I expect of Paul Karem Mortgage Company

Leadership
I want to work for a leader, not a manager. I want to work for someone who represents his company with pride and integrity. You are the company to our clients. You are the first point of contact as we build relationships with our realtors. You bring in the business.

High Ethical Standards
Honesty with staff and clients. Pride in the business.

Accessible
I can talk to you whenever I need to. To speak openly.

Our *Dreaded* Customer Service Review

(One that BEGS our recent customer
to be brutally honest.)

Help us improve so we can SERVE you better.
Please take a few moments to answer these questions about your recent experience with our company.

On a 1 to 10 scale, with 10 representing the best rating and 1 the worst rating, please respond to the following. If you are unsure about a response, try to err on the side of being too critical.

1. How do you feel about the way our firm handles the telephone? this means call returns, the manner answered, responsiveness, etc. Rating: _____.

2. Please rate the general performance of the following team members: (rate for one, some, or all)
Paul____ Terri_____ Jeanie____ Jo____ Bobbi_____

3. The value of our product. Were our rates and prices attractive? Rating:_____.

4. Did the closing agent provide you with courteous service? Rating:_____.

Additional Comments: _____

_____

_____

_____

_____